Boys Will Be Boys-The Joys and Terrors of Raising Boys

The editors dedicate this anthology to their families, the contributors, the contributors' families, and to God.

The Anthology is made up of twelve writers and stories about boys—Sons-Brothers-Fathers-Nephews-Influential Men. Some of the stories are true, some are fictional, but they all show the joys and terrors of raising boys or the joys and terrors of having boys in the family, no matter their age.

Chapter headings by Cher'ley Grogg, little clips of her son Tom Grogg, as he grew up.

Chapters have Thoughts from Parents- please check with your family pediatrician when in doubt. The authors and editors are not responsible for misinterpreted suggestions.

Aesop's Fables are added at the end of each chapter.

All stories, poems, photographs, word clips, and everything in this anthology are covered by copyright and may not be used in any way without permission of the author, and/or the editor.

Some of the stories are fictional and refer to no real person or place. The editors have left the stories mostly as they were written by the original Contributors.

Chapter One..Dusty Wallace
Chapter Two..Dreama Pritt
Chapter Three..Steve Scott
Chapter Four........................... Theresa Jenner Garrido
Chapter Five...Gloria Alden
Chapter Six... Mike Staton
Chapter Seven...Linda Scott
Chapter Eight...Misty Montega
Chapter Nine ....Maxwell Taylor
Chapter Ten............................... Cher'ley Grogg
Chapter Eleven...Frank Lanerd
Chapter Twelve...Del Grogg

What Little Boys are Made Of
By Robert Southey(1774–1843),

Little Girls are made of
Sugar and Spice and
Everything nice

But,

Little Boys are made of
Snakes and Snails and
Puppy dog tails.

All American Boy

Photo Mitchell
Curtis Hopkins

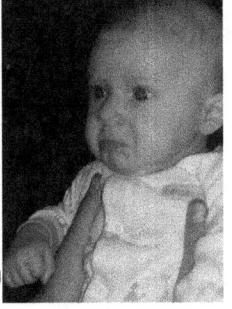

A baby boy comes
In most every size
With mischievous face
And questioning eyes,
With misshapen halo
And a wonderful grin,
With ten busy fingers,
And one sticky chin.
He's cunningly stubborn
And amazingly fast

So you'll never find him
Where you put him last.
He'll keep you so busy,
And yet all the while
Nothing will soften your work
Like his smile,
And no greater treasure
Has brought homes more joy
Than a lovable, dear,
All-American boy.'
~~ Author Unknown ~~

Chapter One

My heart nearly came out of my chest with pride and fear as I gazed on my son. The doctor said, "You have a bouncing baby boy." Immediately I thought Tommy. He received a black eye during the birthing process. Instantly, I knew I was in for an adventure.

By the time, he was 6 months old he was walking around furniture, and he managed to pick up and break a very expensive lion statue I had setting on the middle of the coffee table. Never dreamed he could reach that far in or that he would be strong enough to lift it. Boys should never be underestimated. ~Cher'ley

Dusty Wallace

Dusty lives in the Appalachians of Virginia with his wife and two sons. He enjoys reading, writing, and the occasional fine cigar.

He is the father of two boys, ages 9 and 2, who lives in the Appalachians of southwest Virginia. He was a stellar high-school student which led to being accepted into a decent college. He subsequently squandered that opportunity by being irresponsible and not doing any work. He'd planned on being a writer, but, after dropping out, he feared it would never happen. He's now working on proving himself wrong

Typical Day Off
by Dusty Wallace

8:30 AM - Crispin, my 2 year-old, wakes me by crawling out of bed and turning off my CPAP, a breathing machine to control my apnea. A few gasps later and I'm ready to start the day.

8:45 AM - Diaper changed. Chocolate milk is in a sippy cup, bacon strips in the microwave, biscuits in the oven. I turn on "Curious George."

9:00 AM - Half a biscuit and two strips of bacon are on the floor. Crispin is done eating. A refill of chocolate milk is imminent. His eyes are glued to the television.

9:30 AM - I'm on my fourth cup of coffee. I didn't get home until 1AM from work last night. The end credits roll on "Curious George" and my eyelids are getting heavy.

10:00 AM - Diaper changed again. I have switched Crispin to low sugar apple juice for health and digestive purposes. I put on "Winnie the Pooh."

10:30 AM - Crispin sits on my lap watching Pooh and the gang, except during the musical numbers, in which he slides to the floor to dance.

11:00 AM - Oh dear Lord; it's only 11:00AM? Why? Why can't it be nap time yet? I go to use the restroom, consequences of coffee.

11:05 AM - I come back from the restroom. Crispin is covered in his mother's hand lotion that he found on an end table. Thankfully, he is only in a diaper. I wipe the lotion from his hands, face, belly, legs, and toes. "Finding Nemo" plays in the background.

11:45 AM - He yawns. I yawn, too. Soon it will be time for a nap. The most glorious time of the day, the time when all the problems of the world vanish. I lose track of whatever talking animal is on the T.V.

12:00 PM - I've made it to noon. Noon! Only five hours left until Mommy comes home and saves Daddy from a nervous breakdown. My work schedule calls for four, ten-hour days, Saturday through Tuesday. It's Wednesday through Friday that test my patience.

12:30 PM - Crispin lays in his bed. He'll be asleep soon. I'll just lay here until he doses off, then I'll get things done. There's a whole list of things I need to... Zzzzzzzzzzz

2:00 PM - I'm awake. So is Crispin. It's back to the living room for another round of "Curious George" on Netflix. Microwaveable crispy fries and chicken nuggets should go well with the cartoon. His diaper looks like a Macy's Parade float and horror waits within.

3:00 PM - I dress Crispin in jeans and a "Curious George" t-shirt. It's almost time to multiply my troubles.

3:30 PM - The bell rings. Crispin stares down the hallway as Elijah, his 9 year-old brother approaches. He yells, "Di-ja! Di-ja! Di-ja!"

4:00 PM - The good news: Elijah and Crispin are in his room playing. The bad news: Playing *always* turns to fighting. Elijah likes to boss Crispin around, making him cry. Crispin sees Elijah getting yelled at and realizes that he can get Elijah in trouble by crying. It's a vicious circle.

4:30 PM - Elijah insists that we watch a show on Netflix about guys who build fish tanks. Anything else will not do. Crispin

insists on being fed mini chocolate-chip muffins. I give him the muffins. Elijah sees and demands that he also be given muffins.

All I've had to eat is Crispin's leftover chicken nuggets, so I have some muffins, too.

5:00 PM - Missy, my wife, is getting off work now. She better be home in about a half hour. I go to the restroom and splash some cold water on my face. My reflection shows glassy eyes with dark circles underneath. Screams come from the living room. Probably just horse-play, but I have to check.

5:05 PM - Crispin had taken Elijah's (very expensive) handheld video game system. Elijah pushed him down and yanked it out of his hands. I take the game and send Elijah back to his bedroom for a little quiet time. Crispin I have to hold tight until the tears stop. When they do, he marches right back into his brother's room. I know the peace won't last long.

5:30 PM - The door opens. My beautiful savior of a wife glides across the threshold. I give her the rundown of the day. "Everything's as usual," I say before stretching out on the couch and dozing off.

6:00 - 9:00 PM - Family time. Dinner. Homework. Cartoons.

9:00 PM - It's bed-time for the kiddos. Elijah gets tucked in and kissed on the forehead. Crispin needs Mommy to lay next to him until he's completely unconscious.

9:30 PM - My wife and I talk about our day. We turn on a T.V. show that's *not* animated.

11:30 PM - Bed-time for Mommy and Daddy. Though neither of us say it, we can't help but hope for more days like this. These are the kind of days we never want to forget. The kind of days that make life worth living. Now it's time to dream of cartoon monkeys and recharge our batteries for tomorrow.

The Diet of Seagulls
by Dusty Wallace

A cool, breezy, and overcast day greeted us near the boardwalk of Virginia Beach. It was early March and my wife, and I were in town with our first son, Elijah, visiting an old friend. Swimming wasn't in our itinerary, and no one was in danger of sunburn.

Caring more about food than weather, the ever-present seagulls whirled tornadically overhead. Elijah was only eighteen months old, still sucking on a pacifier. His crystal-blue eyes followed the birds as his wispy corn-silk hair fluttered in the breeze. He was entranced.

My wife held Elijah while I threw a crumb of bread into the sand. Birds swarmed the morsel in Hitchcockian fashion. Having watched closely, Elijah instantly wanted to try the trick himself.

It wasn't long before the bag was empty. Elijah looked at us with those big eyes, his baby-grunts saying, "More!" I raised my hands and showed him the empty bag.

A flash of blue streaked through my peripheral vision. Elijah had thrown his pacifier; the blue plastic guard lay as a speck in the vast expanse of sand.

To my amazement, a seagull swooped down and grabbed the pacifier like an Owl catching a mouse. He flew off down the beach, and the pacifier was never seen again.

Elijah smiled and puffed out his tiny chest with pride. It was only during the walk back to our hotel that realization struck him. He no longer had a pacifier. He cried at his loss.

The mourning lasted until Mommy, and I bought another at the store that evening.

It was a happy ending for all.

The Boys and the Frogs
An Aesop's Fable

Some boys, playing near a pond, saw a number of Frogs in the water, and began to pelt them with stones.

They killed several of them, when one of the Frogs, lifting his head out of the water, cried out:

"Pray stop, my boys; what is sport to you is death to us."

Moral of Aesops Fable: What we do in sport often makes great trouble for others.

Thoughts from Parents

It's okay to mourn your old life and think, "Dear God what have we done!"

You'll shower with the curtain open, do silly dances, make silly faces, and sing silly songs about bodily functions.

Ask for help. Accept help when offered.

Upset? Will what you are upset about be important in five years or even in five hours.

You're not a bad mom or dad if you don't love every single bit of child-rearing.

It's important to spend at least a few hours a week on something other than changing diapers. Take some time away from the baby.

Don't try to accomplish too much in a day.

It's perfectly acceptable to abandon a shopping cart full of groceries if your baby is fussy.

Cry if you need to, and allow yourself to be tired.

Take a moment, recharge, and bury your face in your baby boy's neck.

Walk with the baby. Even it's just to the corner or around the block. Nothing bonds a parent and child better than fresh air.

This too shall pass. This little saying will get you through a lot of situations.

You're a good mom and dad if you're doing your best. Don't let anyone tell you otherwise.

The days are long, but the years are short.

Therefore do not worry about tomorrow, for tomorrow will worry about itself. Each day has enough trouble of its own. (Matthew 6:34)

Chapter Two

From an early age Tommy was a bit rebellious, a bit being defined like an open fire is a bit hot. During the "terrible twos", he threw little temper tantrums and we often had a power struggle going on. I usually won, but there was a couple of times that he had a good enough argument that I knew he'd grow to be a lawyer. (He did not.)~Cher'ley

Dreama Pritt

When Dreama Pritt was in Elementary School, she looked up at visiting poet Muriel Miller Dressler in wide-eyed wonder, thinking "I want to be a writer too."

Now a Marshall University graduate and graduate assistant teaching English Composition , she is a Maier Award-winning author whose publishing credits include *Biostories*, *Ft Cetera* and *Christianity Today's SmallGroups.com*. Her scholarly work often inhabits the intersection of literature and religious studies, and she has received awards and publications in multiple genres, including poetry, fiction, and creative nonfiction. She has been married to MU Alumnus Bill Pritt since 1989, and they have three brilliant and witty children. Dreama is a native West Virginian, who was cradled by mountains and is still delighted with lightning bugs.

Brotherly Love
by Dreama Pritt

On the day, my parents brought me home from the hospital; my brother Terry ran the mile from the bus stop at the mouth of the holler so he could be the first to hold me. With his twelve year old lanky legs at full speed in the snow, breath jaggedly steaming; he made it to the house ahead of our two oldest brothers. In the moment commemorated on film, I look like an Eskimo baby, thick black hair surrounded by a baby blue blanket with bunnies. Terry's face is covered with a silly smile that outshines his silver eye patch. (He lost his eye to a firecracker less than a month before. Mom said that it took four grown men to hold him down so the doctor could examine him.) From that day on, we had a special relationship. Our other brothers were traveling the world with the Army by the time I was four, so I didn't get to know them very well until I was older. Terry, though, was a constant in my life. The year I went to Kindergarten; he was a high school senior—and my school bus guardian. When I tripped and smashed my nose on a walkway grating (because I was running to watch *The Wizard of Oz*'s annual television appearance), he picked me up and carried me home, my blood and snot and tears staining his Army-green field jacket.

Don't imagine, though, that he took no delight in tormenting his baby sister. When I was learning to walk, he'd toss a pillow at my knees to knock me down. He'd stick his finger in peanut butter, pretend to pick his nose, and then lick the peanut butter off, relishing "eatin' boogers". (I wonder, if this is why I have always hated peanut butter?) He'd tuck a sliver of carrot in his fist, swim his hand through the fish bowl, pop the carrot in his mouth and crunch the bones of the "goldfish." He told me that I was *born just to wash the dishes*. Tormenting me, I think, was one of his favorite pastimes. Until one day, when my childhood guilelessness ended at least one of his favorite pranks for a good long time.

***

Terry is taking a nap in the living room, teenaged limbs sprawled across the white and black houndstooth couch; his right arm covering his eyes. At four, years old, I've shed the newborn

Eskimo look. Black hair now blonde; scrunched up eyes now wide. I step gently across the red carpet.

I like the way it feels under my bare feet. I sit on the coffee table, kicking my legs. I sigh. *I wish Terry would wake up. He's fun.* My nose is bugging me. My tiny little finger pulls out a huge snot-covered booger. Now my nose feels better, but I don't know what to do with the booger. *Wait! Terry likes to eat them! I don't want it. Ewww.* Sliding off the table, I lean over and proudly, joyfully put the whole booger in my big brother's mouth.

Less than a second from deep sleep to sitting up and sputtering, Terry is really, really mad. *WHAT DID YOU DO THAT FOR?*

Huge tears overflow. I don't understand why he's yelling. He eats boogers ALL the time. I thought he'd be happy. *But, you said you liked them.*

***

During my brother's sabbatical from being the boogie man, I discovered that my mother was *the tooth fairy for the whole wide world!* But, that is another story.

Photo: Jack Alexander Pritt, trying on his father's army hat. It was taken in our on post housing at Fort Bragg, NC.

Whirlwind
By Dreama Pitt

Blustery breezes turn the
freshly sprung leaves;
Treacherous clouds, teal-green
with warning,
cover the once blue sky.
Sirens sound, and the young
man abandons weed-tending
for a dash inside.
Shooing his sisters to safety,
taking the stairs two steps
at a time, his heart races
with purpose, not fear.

The danger receded,
the basement-emerged trio
discovers the abandoned
weed-eater has wept
gasoline tears on
the living room carpet.

Photo: it is a photo of Dreama's brother tossing her daughter into the air. He taught her to call him "Uncle Terry Goodlookin'," and he would only throw her into the air if she called him that when she asked. It was taken at my parents' farm in Mason County, WV.

The Mischievous Dog
An Aesop's Fable

A Dog used to run up quietly to the heels of those he met, and to bite them without notice. His master sometimes suspended a bell about his neck, that he might give notice of his presence wherever he went, and sometimes he fastened a chain about his neck, to which was attached a heavy clog, so that he could not be so quick at biting people's heels.

The Dog grew proud of his bell and clog, and went with them all over the market-place. An old hound said to him: "Why do you make such an exhibition of yourself? That bell and clog that you carry are not, believe me, orders of merit, but, on the contrary, marks of disgrace, a public notice to all men to avoid you as an ill-mannered dog."

Moral of Aesops Fable: Those who achieve notoriety often mistake it for fame.

Thoughts from Parents

Mom will hold her son close and slow dance with him in her kitchen, thinking: "I will be the one to teach you how to dance before you dance with a little girl in Junior High. Then one day in the far-far future you will be all grown up, taller than me, and we will dance at your wedding."

From the moment they come bouncing into your bed at 5:30 in the morning until they pass out at bedtime, boys go. They only have two speeds -- fast and faster.

Mom's heart will melt the first time she sees Daddy holding her son. And again, as they toss the tiny football. Later they will be high-fiving, fist-bumping, laughing together, or just kicking back, she will get great pleasure in watching the father and son together.

Correct your child as soon as they start crawling. Do not let them pull things from the stand for their safety and your sanity, you will be so proud when you take him to visit the in-laws.

There Will Be Planes, Trains and Automobiles. You may do as I did and stock your nursery with mixed-gender toys like baby dolls and My Little Pony, but your little boy will find the one wheeled toy and play with it nonstop. Little boys adore anything that flies, sails, drives, digs or mixes.

You've heard about the Terrible Two's, but you may be unprepared for this rite of passage. Your little angel may instantly become a little imp. It doesn't begin exactly on your child's second birthday. It can strike as early as 18 months and as late as 30 months, or possibly not at all—(Right). Watch for assertiveness from your toddler. Behaviors to watch for: He may insist on doing exactly what you've told him not to do or throw himself down on the floor in a fit of temper if he doesn't get his way. He'll probably likely ask for something that he doesn't even want, just to see if he has enough power to get it. Find a way to control this early in his life. Perhaps hold him on your lap until he settles down.

Listen, my son, to your father's instruction and do not forsake your mother's teaching. They are a garland to grace your head and a chain to adorn your neck. (Proverbs 1:8,9)

Chapter Three

At three years old, Tommy loved to eat dirt. Actually it was sand. I took him to the doctor and asked if there was something missing from his diet. The doctor said probably not. He said he probably just liked the taste of the sand. That sure made me feel great. I kept a close eye on him and gave him other things to snack on, eventually he outgrew his desire for sand. ~Cher'ley

Steve Scott

Steve Scott's mom somehow knew he was going to be a writer from a very young age. It took him about 15 more years to figure that out, however. After realizing in college that math was "not his thing," he chose a major that allowed him to completely avoid it — and graduated with an English degree from Jacksonville State University in the early 90s. Since then, he's pursued his dreams of corporate mediocrity by working in advertising and crafting ads for a variety of national clients, including AT&T, Citibank, CDW and BlueCross BlueShield. When not writing ads or tales of woe about his personal life, Steve plays drums in a Psychedelic Surf Metal band.

You can contact Steve at steve@iwritegood.net

Father-Son Bonding
By Steve Scott

Not sure what made it pop into my head, but this is a story about something that happened a few years ago. It was when I was still living in Dallas, and my sons Zeb and Stephen were staying with me for part of the summer. At the time, they were about eight and six, respectively. Along with juggling work and parenting, I was trying to do as many fun things with them as I could in the short time we had together. Since money was tight, it was sometimes a challenge finding new and interesting stuff to do.

Then an opportunity presented itself: baseball tickets. One of our print production people at work had gotten Rangers tickets through a vendor (print production people always get all the good boondoggles), and she was kind enough to throw them my way.

Okay, I'm not much of a sports fan. That's actually a bit of an understatement. I have no interest in sports whatsoever. I'm completely lacking that inherited male gene that makes men enjoy watching other men run around chasing balls in tight clothes. I just don't get it. But taking your son or sons to a baseball game? That's a rite of passage. It's Americana. They write songs and make movies about it for goodness' sake. Here was my chance to create a moment my sons would remember for the rest of their lives. They'd talk about it fondly long after I've shuffled off this mortal coil. This was going to be special.

When I got the tickets, the game was still a few days away. I didn't tell the boys what we'd be doing, only that I had "an awesome surprise" for them. I talked it up really big. I mean I really promoted it. I even used it to keep them in line ("if you don't behave, you won't get the awesome surprise I have for you!").

The day before the game, I picked up the boys from their summer day camp, and one of the teachers told me that Zeb had been behaving very poorly for several days — and had even started a fight with one of the other kids. He definitely needed to be punished. My first thought was that he didn't deserve to go to the game. But I couldn't really punish him that way. In doing so, I'd also be punishing Stephen and myself, as well as squashing all the lifelong memories we were going to create! Too much was at stake. So Zeb and I had a very serious talk about how disappointed I was in his behavior, and I told him if I got another bad report the next day, the surprise was off.

Finally, game day arrived. I took the boys back to summer day camp, and reminded them (again) about the surprise I had for them that evening. They were super excited and didn't even know why. I also spoke to Zeb again about his behavior, and reminded him that I'd yank the surprise if he misbehaved. But the truth was there was no way I was going to back out. I was also way too excited. I just had to trust that my "threat" was enough and I wouldn't have to follow through (note to future parents: it usually isn't).

The workday dragged on and on, but finally it was time to go! I hopped in the car and raced to go get the boys. When I got to summer day camp, I asked Zeb's teacher how he'd been. The response I got was, "better, but still not good." The proper thing to do would have been to make good on my punishment. But as I'm sure I made clear that wasn't really an option. Zeb won that round. An example of my parenting skills at their finest.

But screw that! It was time to go to the game! They got in the car with me and asked me a thousand times where we were going. I stayed mum. As we got closer, the kids were smart enough to start looking for signs — I knew they'd figure it out soon. Okay, here's where I have to tell you a little about the layout of Dallas. Rangers Ballpark is in a suburb called Arlington. Also in Arlington, right next to the ballpark, just happens to be another major attraction. That's when they saw the sign. "OH MY GOD! WE'RE GOING TO SIX FLAGS!!!.!" Yes, Six Flags over Texas is right across the street. It had never occurred to me that they'd see the signs for the amusement park and assume that was our destination. As we pulled into the ballpark parking lot, I quickly corrected them and told them that we were not going to Six Flags, but were doing something better. Then one of them (I forget which) saw the Rangers sign and asked if we were going to a baseball game, to which I excitedly responded, "yes! Isn't that awesome?.!" Then they both replied, "can we go to Six Flags instead? PLEASE?" I explained that the surprise all along was that we were going to our first baseball game together, and were going to have a great time. They asked again if we could go to Six Flags instead. Oh boy. I told them no, and asked them to give the game a chance. I knew once we got inside the spectacle of the event would win them over.

The tickets the print production person gave me were primo. They included valet parking, and the best seats I've ever had at any sporting event. We were right behind home plate, just a few rows back. It was a beautiful evening, and the temperature was just right. It was actually really fantastic. It wasn't long until we were seated and experiencing all the sights, sounds and smells of the game. And I was certainly giving the boys the full treatment. We got hot dogs, sodas, big foam fingers, baseball caps, the works. I spent a small fortune on goodies. I was going to make this an occasion to remember if it killed me.

But the boys couldn't get over the disappointment of not going to Six Flags. It was clear that they weren't going to enjoy themselves at the game. No amount of enthusiasm on my part was going to help. I kept trying to get them excited, and at one point asked them, "isn't this fun? Aren't we having a good time?" That's when Stephen responded with an answer I will never forget. He turned to me, looked me right in the eye, and with all seriousness replied, "Worst. Surprise. Ever."

I managed to keep them there through three innings, and we left at the top of the fourth. That's all they could stand. We got in the car and quietly drove home. And so ended my father-son bonding experience. Well... at least one of us will remember it for a lifetime.

Offering The Black Jellybean
By Steve Scott

When we were kids, my brother Ken and I both got a package of jellybeans for Easter. He, like me, LOVES the black ones. Well this particular package that Ken got only had one black jellybean in it. Basically, Ken got hosed. But being the happy-go-lucky kid he was, he decided to focus on the positive. He proceeded to make a big production about how he was SO looking forward to that black jellybean, and how he was going to save it for last and enjoy it SO MUCH when he got to it. We were in the car when this happened, by the way. So he got down to the end of the package, and all he had left was the lone black jellybean. He, wanting to show how kind and generous and selfless he was, stuck it in my dad's face and offered it to him. My dad meanwhile was fighting traffic and not paying attention to Ken's shenanigans in the back seat. He saw the proffered jellybean, said, "sure, thanks," and unceremoniously snatched it from Ken's hand and ate it. It took about 5 seconds for the shock to hit him, but once it did, Ken started crying – and he continued to cry for roughly the next 2-3 hours.

The jellybean was not offered so my dad could really take it, but so he could refuse. You see sometimes, like Ken, a person will make an offer because he or she really only wants to be recognized for the kindness and generosity of the gesture. And also sometimes, like my dad, the other person doesn't catch that it's a hollow offer and doesn't realize he or she wasn't REALLY supposed to accept it. This leads to hurt and confusion

on both ends. In short, you should never offer something you're not truly willing to give. Ken and I BOTH learned a valuable lesson on that fateful Easter day. Although his lesson was slightly more painful than mine; I still got all my black jellybeans.

To this day, when I suspect someone of offering something they're not willing to give, I'll refer to it as "offering the black jellybean." Now you know why.

The Tortoise and the Birds
An Aesop's Fable

A Tortoise desired to change its place of residence, so he asked an Eagle to carry him to his new home, promising her a rich reward for her trouble. The Eagle agreed and seizing the Tortoise by the shell with her talons soared aloft.

On their way they met a Crow, who said to the Eagle: "Tortoise is good eating." "The shell is too hard," said the Eagle in reply. "The rocks will soon crack the shell," was the Crow's answer; and the Eagle, taking the hint, let fall the Tortoise on a sharp rock, and the two birds made a hearty meal of the Tortoise.

Moral of Aesops Fable: Never soar aloft on an enemy's pinions

Thoughts from Parents

Rough play nourishes a child's sensory system through feelings of pressure to their muscles, joints and skin. Boys cannot learn these skills by watching TV or reading a book.

Roughhousing is Dad, Uncle, or Grandpa time. There's the jumping off furniture, landing on each other, rolling around on the floor, slaps on the back, and the "hug" that turns into a full-body slam. Play fighting is hard-wired into many boys. It's often how they connect and express affection.

With boys the rules come early and roughhousing is a place that needs rules:
1. No biting, scratching or kicking
2. No hitting or attacking anyone's head
3. Stop when the other child (or a parent) says "stop."

Boys can jump off the bed, climb out of the crib, hurdle the sofa. You will learn to anticipate the most dangerous risks), but there will be a time when you're just a second too late, and you land up driving to the ER. Don't blame yourself -- it's a rite of passage for the Mom of boys.

You should buy corner protectors, cabinet locks, and those little socket covers.

To burn energy take your kids to a nearby playground or park where they can let loose, scream, yell, and release themselves without so many restrictions. After a stint of running and boisterous behavior, you can go home for a nice nap.

Boys love their mothers. There's a strong and consistent love that comes from boys from the get-go -- and stays there through the long haul.

My son, if sinful men entice you, do not give in to them. If they say, "Come along with us; let's lie in wait for innocent blood, let's ambush some harmless soul. (Proverbs 1: 10, 11a)

Chapter Four

At four years old, fishing became Tommy's favorite thing to do, especially with his grandpa and grandma. I'd take him berry picking and walking along a country creek. One time as a group of us were walking up a creek bed, he said, "Snake." We walked a little farther, and Tommy again said, "Snake." I didn't pay too much attention because he'd been having horrible nightmares about snakes.

He woke up one night screaming and screaming. "Get them off me. Get them off me."

I asked, "What?"

He cried, "Snakes. Snakes are all over me."

I cradled him and assured him there were no snakes on him. Finally he fell back to sleep, but he had that reoccurring dream for several months.
~Cher'ley

Theresa Jenner Garrido

Born and raised in the beautiful Pacific Northwest, Theresa Jenner Garrido spent the first nine years of her life on an island in Puget Sound, off the coast of Washington State. She attended the University of Washington, received a B.A. in English, and spent the next twenty-plus years teaching middle school language arts, social studies, and drama before retiring "early". Now Theresa is happy to indulge her wild imagination and passionate love of history—rooted in a deep faith in God, and share these foibles and gifts with others, including her husband, her ever-growing family, a rescue pup and the stray black cat who rules the house.

Theresa has made her home in Missouri, Georgia, and North Carolina but currently resides in South Carolina. When not at the computer or in the laundry room, she enjoys traveling and poking her nose into strange and mysterious places. Because of this, each one of her books is based on an event that actually happened.*http://www.amazon.com/author/theresagarrido*
htto://http://www.booksbytheresa.vpweb.com

THE COLLECTION
By Theresa Jenner Garrido

When my older sister's husband accepted a new job in rural Missouri, I was devastated. Her kids were my kids, so it wasn't too long before I packed my bags and followed. Lucky enough to find a teaching position in a town nearby, this Pacific Northwest gal settled in nicely.

Living only a mile down the road—a winding road, lined with splendid oaks, cow pastures, and corn fields—I was close enough to spend half my waking hours at my sister's house. She cooked better than I, and her six boys and one girl were the heart and soul of my existence. I had been a tomboy growing up and loved being around boys because they played way better games. If my boy cousins weren't around, then I would follow my dad everywhere. We'd take long walks in the woods, spend hours in the boat on Puget Sound, and would backpack every summer in the Olympic Mountains or the Cascades. I was a natural, therefore, to oversee my nephews' summer activities.

I loved the outdoors, thrived on books about American history and the lives of our early settlers, and devoured anything to do with Native Americans—especially the Blackfeet. So with that foundation, it was natural for me to devise intricate games and challenges for my six nephews. They collected feathers and leaves, rocks and berries—anything that focused on Mother Nature—and catalogued their discoveries in spiral notebooks. Each one could name every tree and leaf around and identify every bird and its call. My sister was happy to have me take over during the summer months because busy, engaged boys meant fewer incidences and naughty pranks.

Or so we naively thought.

Even with two "mothers" on site, my six nephews managed to set intricate traps for wild animals and only succeeded in trapping one another. They tested rope strength by tying the youngest to a tree and then "forgetting" him for hours. They constructed tree forts that collapsed—resulting in several miracles, seeing no bones were ever broken. They threw rocks, persimmons and anything else moderately round and throw-able and only broke one window—that we were aware of.

The boys had two dogs that were their constant companions and partners in crime. Maggie, a ladylike collie, who did her best to babysit, and Missi—short for Mississippi Mud— a mixed-breed who, we believe, was the mastermind behind most of the crimes.

Dave, the oldest, delighted in terrorizing his younger siblings. Once he taped the sound of wire hangers moving and clicking, and then hid the tape recorder in his younger brothers' closet. Set to begin playing after the boys were tucked into bed, and lights were off, this prank proved very successful and had the little boys, leaping out of bed or clawing their way under covers, amid shrieks of terror.

Pete, second in line, and nicknamed "Sweet Pete" by his elders, did his best to dissuade his older brother from traumatizing the little ones but found it an exhausting feat.

Dan, our "Mr. Spock," enjoyed the games and shenanigans but could take or leave them and often out-witted big brother, Dave—much to Pete's satisfaction.

Matt and Andy, the youngest, were often in a world of their own—preferring to go it alone rather than trying to keep up with the older four.

It was Joe—fourth in line—who had the greatest challenges to overcome. A typical "middle child," Joe was too young for Dave, Pete and Dan, and too old for Matt and Andy. That meant Joe tried harder.

And succeeded in getting into more mischief than we ever expected a skinny, knobby-kneed little boy with a gamin grin could create.

One incident remains forever fresh in my mind. My sister wanted something from the large pantry kept in the daylight basement. I happily skipped downstairs and was passing the big room set up as a dormitory for the four older boys. Taking up one end of the house, it contained two sets of bunk beds, four dressers, a huge closet and the million-and-one assorted paraphernalia that most young boys delight in.

No lights were on, and the room was in shadow, but a glimpse of something struck a nerve. Something strange was lined up on Joe's dresser. Something I instinctively knew shouldn't be there. So I entered the room, switched on the light and stared at the unexpected.

Six very large, very hairy brown mice lay on their tummies in neat military formation. Six pairs of very black, very sightless round eyes stared back at me. On closer examination—I nudged one with a pencil—I discovered, to my creeping unease, that each of the creatures had long ago passed to that cheese factory in the sky, were now quite stiff, but, thankfully, and for a reason I, an English major and not science oriented, could not fathom, did not stink to high heaven.

All that aside, I didn't want to be the one responsible for their relocation, so I called up to my sister, who, happily and blissfully unaware, worked in her kitchen. "Susan?" I yelled. "Hey, Susan?"

"You calling me?" she answered.

"Oh, yeah. Joe's got something down here I'm not sure he should have."

"He does? What?"

"Well, he's got a pretty nice collection going here, on top of his dresser."

"Well, what is it? I'm busy."

"Mice."

"What?"

"Mice. Joe's got six very dead, very stiff mice, lined up on his dresser."

My sister's resounding shriek for my brother-in-law put an abrupt end to our dialogue. With a grin, I headed for the pantry to retrieve the item she'd sent me to fetch.

Tomorrow would be another day with another adventure. No telling what Dave would instigate or what dear Joe would collect.

I knew, with satisfaction, it would be interesting.

These are 5 of Theresa's nephews all grown up. She feels so blessed to have always been a part of their lives and she still is.

Theresa said, "After rejoicing in my six nephews, whom I cherished as my own, and watching them grow from rambunctious boys into stalwart young men, I wrote this poem. This is dedicated to David, Peter, Dan, Joe, Matt and Andy. What amazing men you've become."

Boy Song
By Theresa Jenner Garrido

I took such joy in watching them.
They played so hard
And filled the yard
With laughter, shouts,
And so much noise.
Those naughty, precious
Little boys.
From morning until setting sun,
They never stopped
To sleep or rest.
They had such zest
For life.
And lived each minute;
Used it well,
And I would not have guessed
That they would grow
To be so tall.
I hear them still
In dreams at night.
I see them at their play.
Wasn't it just yesterday?
Those precious, naughty
Little boys,
Where have those years all gone?
Their laughter echoes
Hauntingly
And sings
Its own sweet song.

PLEASE, LORD, GIVE ME A CLASSROOM FULL OF BOYS...I THINK
By Theresa Jenner Garrido

Dear, Lord, please give me a classroom full of boys, was my mantra before the start of each new school year. I had grown up with boy cousins and was fully involved in the raising of my sister's six boys. I knew and appreciated boys, and twenty-plus years as a middle school teacher only reinforced that. Dealing with boys was just plain easier than dealing with the mood swings and capriciousness of the female gender, even though I was one, myself. And besides, I'd passed the test; endured the crucible; had been baptized with fire...and come out alive.

My love affair began my second year as a teacher. Fresh out o f university, with only one year's experience under my belt, this Seattle girl applied for a teaching position in a small school in rural Missouri—smack dab in the middle of farm country. And to anyone who knows farming that meant a classroom full of healthy, robust students, used to baling hay, mucking barns, and driving heavy machinery long before their sixteenth birthday. In short: big, burly man-boys, whom I would have to persuade to sit still for hours at a time, in hard, wooden desks that could barely accommodate their five-foot eight to over six-foot muscular, long-legged bodies.

I was hired to teach fifth through eighth grade language arts. And, again, if you know anything at all about the male of our species at that age—never mind whether from city or country— that translated into an almost insurmountable task. I, the petite "newbie" would be demanding that they, the hardened, earthy adolescents, enjoy such phrases as *I wandered lonely as a cloud*

That floats on high o'er vales and hills (William Wordsworth). You think?

I remember the first day as if it were yesterday. It comprised of meeting and greeting, taking down names, explaining the curriculum, and generally getting acquainted. I went home that afternoon feeling like one of Wordsworth's clouds. I was meant to be a teacher. I had been called—like missionaries of the Past—and would succeed in broadening young minds and enriching young lives. That is if I didn't become permanently disabled from craning my neck in order to look at faces, towering a good seven inches above me.

The second day is cemented into my memory, as well, but for a very different reason. The annals of history will forever mark it as the first day of my trial by fire.

I entered the classroom that second morning in high spirits. I put away purse and lunch in the cupboard and sat down at my desk. I opened my lesson plan book, scanned what I'd written then went out to the hallway to wait for my seventh graders. In minutes, the hall filled with noisy, jostling students, and my chest swelled with pride as I shared smiles and nods with my fellow teachers, also waiting at their doors. In groups of twos and threes, the boys and girls entered my classroom, stashed their lunches and book bags in the cloak area at the back of the room then took their seats. The bell rang, signaling the day's start, and I walked to my desk, sat, and opened the attendance book.

A few snickers should have cued me that trouble was simmering, and I admit it did raise a few hairs at the back of my neck, but ingénue that I was, I ignored them. Two minutes later and only half-way through roll, I noticed a small box on my desk, behind my hefty dictionary, which I hadn't seen earlier.

Reaching for it, my hand paused when a ripple of smothered giggles ran through the group like wind through the tall grass in the pasture outside my window. I glanced up, but the class sat still, and all eyes were glued on me. Now, not only the hairs at the back of my neck stood on end, but both arms tickled, too.

I smiled. "Did somebody bring me a present?" Three snorts and a snicker. "That's so nice. Thank you."

I lifted the lid and peered inside. Two round, viscous orbs stared back at me.

Eyes. Cow's eyes. Lying, pretty as you please, in a cardboard shoebox.

Naïve "newbie" or not, I knew instinctively that if I betrayed my abhorrence and disgust I'd be treated to these "gifts" for the rest of the year. So I smiled, tilted the box so the others could see inside—resulting in shrill squeals from the girls and more sniggers from the boys—and said, "How cool! I've never seen eyeballs out of their sockets before. Too bad I don't teach science, or we could have fun dissecting these. Whoever brought them—thanks." Then I replaced the lid and held the box out to the nearest boy—a brawny lad who just happened to be wearing the smirkiest of smirky grins.

"Dale, would you take this out to the dumpster, please?" I chirped prettily. "Unfortunately, we don't have a refrigerator in here so they won't keep. We don't want to stink up our room." Dale accepted the box without a word, disappeared out the door and returned in less than five minutes. The rest of the day went by with no further surprises.

Day three, however, was another matter. The third day of my year at this new school became day two of my ordeal. The students got settled; I took attendance and class began. Twenty minutes into first period, I needed something from the bottom drawer of my desk. I pulled open the large drawer only to find a burlap sack instead of the folders I'd expected to see. Now already a seasoned veteran after only twenty-four hours, thanks to yesterday's initiation, I prepared my psyche for something equally nasty. Or even worse.

It was worse. Opening the bag, I saw to my utter horror, a nice, plump, over-two-feet long black snake, curled at the bottom. I hated snakes. With a passion, I hated snakes. Like *Indiana Jones*, I hated snakes. Snakes were one of the reoccurring dreams   that plagued me since childhood.

Slowly, so as not to betray any adverse emotion, I closed the bag and smiled out at my waiting-on-tenterhooks class. "Well, this is probably one of the silliest gifts I've gotten yet. Like I said yesterday, too bad I'm not the science teacher. Oh, well...guess there aren't that many dead poets lying on the road...so, why not a snake? Right?" Of course, at the mention of "snake" the girls moaned and squeaked and pulled their feet up, but the boys just

beamed. Then in a deja vu pantomime of yesterday, I handed
the sack to Dale, he dutifully left his seat and transported the
nasty business to the dumpster behind the school. When he
returned, the class resumed its study of nouns and verbs and the
sun set without incident on the second day of my crucible.

Needless to say, I went to school the following morning with
tickles of apprehension running up and down my back. Cow's
eyes, road kill snake—what would my boys think of next?

Like a well-choreographed dance, my morning routine began
as it should, and first period started on time. Feelings of relief
trickled into my tense mind, and I'd almost convinced myself that
the test was over, when I heard a faint scratching noise coming
from my top desk drawer. For some reason, I hadn't opened that
drawer yet for anything. Now, fully convinced that another
delight awaited me, I hesitated before pulling it open a crack to
see what made the noise. Prepared for another snake, I slowly
pulled the drawer open and saw what had to be the biggest
spider this side of the Amazon, scurrying around in circles over
assorted pens, pencils and paper clips.

This demanded an Academy Award Performance and not a
second to prepare or a script to follow. Either by the grace of
God, true grit or dumb luck, I picked up the mammoth, eight-
legged arachnid by one leg, held it out far from my body—
accompanied by the anticipated shrieks from the girls and the
guffaws from the boys—and swiftly and deftly conveyed the
creature to the open window. With a flick of a wrist, it was gone,
lost among the shrubbery beneath my first floor window.

On the outside, I was cool, calm and collected—with just a
pinch of disdain to give credence to my indifference. On the
inside, however, I writhed and squirmed and squealed louder
than any of the seventh grade girls, who sat there, with mouths,
agape and eyes, wide with acute horror.

My next words should have been recorded in some hall of
fame or, at the very least, have accorded me the Medal of Honor.
I leaned against my desk, crossed my arms and said with
composure and a yawn, "Open your books to page eleven and
start on exercise one. We'll exchange papers in fifteen minutes."

Then I sat at my desk, took out a tissue and blew my nose.
Not because I needed to, but to give me something to hide

behind for a second while I collected the splinters of a fractured equilibrium.

I received one more "gift" that week. I survived that one, too, I am happy to say, and, therefore, can proudly proclaim to one and all that by October, I had every single one of the boys, eating out of my hand. While the girls continued to gossip and pass notes and descend into acute despair and rise up, only to crash again and again, the boys and I had a pretty tolerable year, despite the times we had to read such whimsical stuff like "The Daffodils" by William Wordsworth.

So, yes, I can truthfully say, "Lord, please give me a classroom of boys."

A boy is like a Kite
By Theresa Jenner Garrido

I hold the string tightly in both hands,
Battling the strong wind.
The kite, twisting and turning, fights;
Pulls hard to break free.
Like a crazed animal, trapped,
The kite bites.
How do I tame it?
I tug on the string.
I frantically wrap it around the spool.
If I tighten the rein gently, the kite will comply.
But, if I bring it in too close, too taut,
It will die.
If I give it too much slack, too much string, too much freedom,
I will lose it forever.
O wild kite!
So like my son, you are!
How awesome is the wisdom of discipline.

Recipe for a Nightmare
By Theresa Jenner Garrido

Take one big brother, plus two additional brothers who back up big brother, add a rural setting, mix in enough sightings of spider webs-in-the-making and bleeding squirrels and assorted road-kill, stir slowly for several days until well set. The perfect nightmare recipe for one four-year-old boy.

When my sister, brother-in-law and their seven kids—six boys and one girl—moved to Missouri, I soon followed. Single and relatively free to uproot, it didn't matter to me where I lived as long as it was close to what I considered my kids. Luck and the grace of God was with me because not only did I find the perfect teaching position in a town ten miles down the highway, I was able to snag a cozy over-the-garage apartment on a farm only a mile down the country road from where my sister's family lived. This was important for several reasons. One, of course, was that I wanted to be close enough to join in family activities. Two, my sister and brother-in-law needed all the additional help they could get, minding six rambunctious boys and one girl who was lost in the middle.

David, the eldest, was The Instigator. He was a ringleader beyond all ringleaders; a mastermind of such incredible feats of mischief that I wouldn't be surprised to discover he'd been under scrutiny by the NSA, the CIA and every other clandestine federal organization when he was a youth. Dave was that good. He was the brother that planned the pranks, exquisitely designed to torment the younger siblings. The next two in line, Pete and Dan, while not officially in cahoots, at least kept silent. There were no stool pigeons or squealers among them.

So, with that knowledge tucked at the back of my mind, I was not too surprised one night while tucking in four-year-old Joe to find him cowering in bed with the covers drawn up to his chin.

"Okay, buddy, say your prayers," I said, gently pulling the covers down. His sweet little face scrunched up and his eyes blinked rapidly. Didn't take a rocket scientist to know he was worried about something.

"So, what's going on in that head of yours?" I tweaked his nose.

"I don't wanna go to sleep," the little guy murmured, gripping his battered Teddy bear close.

"Why not? You've had a pretty long day, kiddo." His face scrunched even more. "Can you tell me why you don't want to go to sleep? It's past your bedtime. Mommy and Daddy let you stay up later. You need your sleep."

"But..."

"But?"

His arm wriggled free from the confines of the blanket and he held out his hand—the hand that bore the neon-bright *Flintstones* Band-Aid across the back.

"You want me to kiss your hand? Does the cut still hurt?" He shook his head but continued to hold the injured hand up. "Joe, sweetie, you have to tell me so I can help you."

"What'f I bleeded in the night?"

"Bleeded? Oh, honey, your cut won't bleed anymore. It wasn't that deep and we put a Band-Aid on it. See? No more blood. Good as new."

His eyes got rounder. "But Dave said..."

Now we were onto something. Red flags waved. I was primed and ready for just about anything. "Go on. But Dave said what?"

"Dave said if my cut bleeded in the night I'd wake up flat."

I choked on the bark of laughter that almost erupted. Instead, I swallowed, coughed, smiled, leaned down to kiss his nose then said, "Did Dave say that? What a silly thing to say. He was just teasing you, Joe. I promise you with my whole heart that you won't bleed all night and wake up flat. And remember, you have a Guardian Angel. Right?" He nodded. "Right. And your Guardian Angel would never ever let you wake up flat. Okay?"

"Okay."

"Good. Now say your prayers."

"But Dave said—"

"Joe...remember when Dave told you if you walked too close to a spider web that the spider would lasso you and wind you up real tight and keep you on her web?"

Joe grinned. "Yeah. You and Mommy said he was a doofus."

I smiled. "Well, something like that. We did laugh, though. Remember?"

"Yeah."

"Why did we laugh?"

"'Cause it wasn't true. Dave was just teasing me."

"Right. And he was teasing you about waking up flat, too. Now say your prayers."

Joe recited his prayers and we even added an extra blessing for Big Brother Dave. God knows, he needed it.

The boys are now grown, but you can't help but wonder if Joe is still being teased.

The Lion and the Mouse
An Aesop's Fable

Once when a Lion was asleep a little Mouse began running up and down upon him; this soon wakened the Lion, who placed his huge paw upon him, and opened his big jaws to swallow him. "Pardon, O King," cried the little Mouse: "forgive me this time, I shall never forget it: who knows but what I may be able to do you a turn some of these days?"

The Lion was so tickled at the idea of the Mouse being able to help him that he lifted up his paw and let him go.

Some time after the Lion was caught in a trap, and the hunters who desired to carry him alive to the King, tied him to a tree while they went in search of a wagon to carry him on.

Just then the little Mouse happened to pass by, and seeing the sad plight in which the Lion was, went up to him and soon gnawed away the ropes that bound the King of the Beasts.

"Was I not right?" said the little Mouse.

Moral of Aesops Fable: Little friends may prove great friends

Thoughts from Parents

Ten Rules to Follow

1. Give him some responsibility.
2. Let him show his emotions.
3. Get involved at his school.
4. Don't try to shut down his high-revving engine.
5. Don't worry if he isn't acting "masculine" enough.
6. Give him chances to express his social skills.
7. Start him playing music early in life.
8. Encourage his interests.
9. Give him plenty of physical affection.
10. Give him lots of praise, and positive attention.

The Silliness Starts Early
There will be days when you watch your son with his friends, and you just won't get it.

Boy humor can be extra goofy and the potty humor starts as soon as they can talk. You will be told that your dinner tastes like poop. You'll be called poopy head and poopy pants. If you laugh (and it's often hard not to) or scold, you just give the poop talk more value.

The Penis Comparisons Also Start Early
Boys play with their penis practically from birth. What's even more shocking: As soon as your little man can speak, the mine-is-bigger-than-your talk starts. Around age 2.5, you'll start to hear things like: "Daddy, your p-p is big." "My p-p is little."

Then comes: "Mommy doesn't have a penis! How does she pee?"

For wisdom will enter your heart, and knowledge will be pleasant to your soul. Discretion will protect you, and understanding will guard you. (Proverbs 2:10,11)

Chapter Five

At five years old, Tommy received his first whipping in Kindergarten. He had refused to go to the reading class. He said he didn't want to go down the stairs. The teacher said, "You go down the stairs to get to go to lunch, and you go down the stairs to go to recess."

Tommy said, "Yes, I have to go to lunch and recess, I don't have to go to reading. The principal took him to the office to give him a spanking. He told him to count the cows on the wallpaper.

Tommy said, "1,2,3,4,5,6..." As fast as he could, until the principal started laughing. He had already given him a couple of swats and let it go at that. Cher'ley

Gloria Alden

Gloria Alden's Catherine Jewell Mystery series are The Blue Rose, Daylilies for Emily's Garden, Ladies of the Garden Club, and a middle-grade book, The Sherlock Holmes Detective Club. Her published short stories include "The Professor's Books" in FISH TALES, The Lure of the Rainbow in FISH NETS, "Once Upon a Gnome" in STRANGELY FUNNY and "Norman's Skeleton's" in ALL HALLOWS EVIL and several stories in the e-zine,

Bethlehem Writers

Roundtable. Her short story "Cheating on Your Wife Can Get You Killed" won the Love is Murder contest in 2011. She blogs every Thursday on Writers Who Kill. She lives on a small farm in NE Ohio with assorted critters, including two ponies, six hens, a barn cat, two house cats, a canary, two ring-necked African Doves and her tricolor collie, Maggie.

http://writerswhokill.blogspot.com/
Website: www.gloriaalden.com

An Accident Waiting to Happen
By Gloria Alden

My second son, Joey, was an accident waiting to happen. Not that I knew that when he was a toddler. In fact, he wasn't as active as my older son, and he loved to be cuddled, rocked and sang to more than his brother, John.

It all started when he was four years old and rolled out of bed breaking his collar bone. He didn't howl and cry much – he never did, but it hurt him when I tried to put his shirt on. That was our first trip to the hospital; the first of many trips. In fact, there were so many I won't be able to remember them in chronological order and maybe not all of them, either.

 Once he hit a football with the back side of a hatchet, and the blade bounced back and hit his forehead. That needed stitches. Another time when I was playing the piano, he came in and told me he thought he broke his wrist. Since he wasn't crying or fussing, I wasn't alarmed and continued to the end of the piece before I asked him if he could wiggle his fingers. He couldn't so another trip to the hospital. One Saturday morning after I brought the kids home from catechism classes at our church, he decided to paint the tree house his brother, and he had built. The spray paint can malfunctioned so he hit the can of green paint with the ax. Fortunately, it was in the tree house and not in the garage. Even more fortunate, the exploding can didn't hit his face or eyes, but the rest of Joey was covered in green paint. Unfortunately, he hadn't changed out of his good clothes, and it went through his good coat, his pants and his shoes. The clothes had to be pitched, and he had green skin for quite some time. That accident didn't require a trip to the hospital. He blamed it on me because I'd told him he could never throw a spray can in a fire, but I'd never told him he couldn't hit it with an ax.

Another time he rode his bicycle down to the corner on our quiet dead end street which was as far as he was allowed to go. He must have hit a rock or something because a neighbor found him lying beside the road unconscious and brought him home. It was another trip to the hospital with a concussion this time.

One of two serious childhood accidents happened the evening before we were leaving for a camping trip to Maine with my parents and some of my siblings still living at home. My in-laws were there to wish us a safe trip. I was sitting in the kitchen talking to them when Joey came in and said that he'd cut his knee. I pulled him up onto my lap, grabbed a dish towel and put it over the knee that was a little bloody, but not excessive. Again, my stoic son wasn't crying or fussing. I think he was seven or eight at the time. Finally, I took him in the bathroom to clean his cut and bandage it. What I saw made me sick. A gash went all the way down to his knee cap. It required numerous stitches inside and out and strict orders to keep it dry. Of course, I tried to see that it was kept dry, but we were camping in Acadia National Park on Maine's seacoast, and the kids had a ball playing in the tide pools, so there were times it got wet. We'd been told to take him in to have his stitches checked in seven days. We went to a doctor the hospital in Bar Harbor recommended, but the doctor refused to get close enough to check the stitches and had his nurse bandage his knee again covering a wound now badly infected. Apparently, in our camping clothes we weren't as important looking as the wealthier people who summered at Bar Harbor in their summer homes or yachts. Our doctor was furious when we went to him as soon as we got home. It took much longer to heal than it would have if that doctor lived by the Hippocratic Oath.

The next serious accident happened when he wasn't much older. My husband was fishing in Canada and due home shortly. We'd just come home from an outdoor art show where I'd been displaying my paintings. The boys decided to surprise their father by cleaning up the branches next to the woods and burning them. I did not know what they were doing. Because they had trouble getting the fire started, Joey went in the garage and filled a small can with white gas we used for our camp stove. When he tossed it on the fire barely started, the flames followed the fumes back and caught his pants on fire. As a den mother, I'd taught them to drop and roll; however, it didn't extinguish the flames, so he got up and ran. John tackled him and brought him down and put the fire out with his hands. John wasn't burned, but Joey was. I wrapped a wet towel around his leg with his polyester pants melted into his skin and took off for the hospital. This was the only time I heard Joey crying and screaming in pain. He was in the hospital for several weeks and required a skin graft. On the day, I took him home; the doctor showed me how to remove the stitches when they were ready to come out and how to care for the skin grafts. I got so nauseated I almost passed out. Joey took care of his own skin graft and removed the stitches when it was time while I handed him the salve and bandages, etc. without looking too closely.

I'd like to say he grew out of being accident prone, but he didn't. As a teenager while riding his horse at a show – not a sedate event, of course, but barrel racing. The ring was quite wet and muddy that day. As Nikki, his palomino, flew across the ring, the cinch broke, and Joe and the saddle ended up under the mare. Fortunately, Nikki stopped, and he wasn't injured, but it was hard to recognize him because of all the mud. I left horse, trailer, and my other kids there, and put him in the back of my pickup and took him home to shower and change.

He had a few automobile accidents and other incidents as a teenager, but I hoped that as he became an adult, all that would be behind him. Not so.

When he was helping me gut an old house I'd bought so he could rewire it to make it safe for me to move into, the water pressure went off. I was going out to prime the well as he'd shown me how the night before, when he said he needed a break from the blown insulation we were shoveling out of the house. When he flipped the electric switch, natural gas in the well house that we knew nothing about, blew him out 20 to 30 feet. His face and chest were blackened as were his arms. His mustache was burned off, and his shirt was in tatters. This was before cell phones, so my daughter ran across the street to get help; I poured what jugs of water I had over his face and chest. He asked me, "Mom, is my face messed up?" I told him no, but I lied. Again he was in the hospital for over a month and out of work. When his wife got to the hospital before the ambulance even got there, she thought he was dead because he was covered with a white sheet.

One of the first things he said to her was, "Thank God it wasn't my mom. She couldn't have stood any more problems." Eventually, the burns healed with only pink skin here and there. He was twenty-six years old, and this should have been the end of his accidents now. After all, he was a responsible, intelligent adult.Not to be. He broke his back several times once it was on a three-wheeled all-terrain vehicle miles from the nearest road. I don't remember how the friend with him got him to the hospital now. Another time he came down off a ladder when he was building his barn. He flipped his truck on a flooded road that had been clear the hour before. The truck ended upside down in a deep ditch, and it was a dark night. Somehow he managed to crawl out the window, but wasn't sure which direction was up. However, he managed to crawl out of the ditch just as a driver from another car came to his aid. I don't remember if an ambulance came or not.

A little over a year and a half ago, Joe and his wife were on a motorcycle in the west when a woman in a van stopped suddenly in front of him as she tried to make up her mind if she wanted to take that exit of not. He didn't hit her, but only because he laid his Harley down. Both he and his wife were hurt, but he was hurt worse. He had extensive road burns, a broken ankle, cracked ribs and a broken collarbone. I didn't find out about their accident until a friend of his drove the long way out there to bring them home. He didn't want me to worry. Again I was taking this son of mine to the hospital and the doctors for numerous visits. My daughter-in-law wasn't as badly hurt but couldn't drive for a while.

So now my son is fifty years old. All his accidents are behind him. At least I'm keeping my fingers crossed since he's an electrician working on cranes often high in the air. He also still rides a motorcycle in nice weather. He hasn't had an accident in a year and a half now. Maybe my little boy has finally grown up. My fingers are crossed, of course.

**

When my husband suffered from midlife crises after almost thirty-one years of marriage and left me, I bought a small farm with an old house in terrible shape. The roof leaked; two basement walls were collapsing with wild critters living there. The house hadn't been painted in thirty or forty years, and the electrical wiring was installed in 1917. So my twenty-six year old son, Joe, started tearing out walls to rewire the house and replace basement walls needing rebuilt. He dry walled the house inside and installed new kitchen cupboards and counters, refinished the floors and so many other things to make it livable and comfortable.

Awhile back, I found the children's book *LOVE YOU FOREVER* written by Robert Munsch, a book starting with a mother rocking her newborn son in her arms, progressing through his growing up years and ending with the son holding his aging mother in his arms and later his own son. I read it to my son when I first discovered it, and it still brings tears when I read it. Following is a poem I wrote for my son about this time.

The Rebuilder
By Gloria Alden

My son has trouble saying
"Thanks, Mom, for
all those balls you threw,
games you attended,
knees you mended."
Instead he repairs
broken locks,
and sump pumps,
fixes drippy faucets,
patches the roof,
the damaged mailbox,
and works to mend
me.

Because my son has trouble saying
"Mom, I love you,"
he pounds nails,
trims rooms, sands floors,
installs cupboards,
new wiring, walls,
and insulation
to warm and protect.
He builds a sunroom
and new steps
for my new life
without a husband.
He works to rebuild
a family.

Saying Good-bye
By Gloria Alden

"The Red Badge of Courage," John said. I tried to see if he had the correct answer to the puzzle on Wheel of Fortune, but I couldn't see through my tears. *I can't say good-bye,* I thought.

Saying good-bye has always been hard for me. When my sisters were leaving for college or friends were moving away, I always dreaded it. I wanted to cling and hold on, but I didn't want to embarrass anyone, so I either avoided the departing person, or made inane jokes, or superficial comments. How much worse this good-bye was the final good-bye.

"Would you stay up and watch TV with me, Mom?" John had asked the night before.

"Of course," I replied. Although I was tired because I'd waited up late for him to come home the night before, I would stay up all night, if necessary, if this was the night to say good-bye.

We sat side by side on the hospital bed we'd had delivered. We held hands as we watched "Benny Hill" then "Dave Alan at Large." It seems strange to me now, but we even laughed and enjoyed those two shows.

Sometime after the late show started, he told me he was tired and would like to sleep. "Would you mind sleeping on the couch?" he asked.

"I planned on it," I replied. As I took my pillow from beside my sleeping husband, I wondered if I should wake him. He, too, would want to say good-bye. I decided against it. There would still be time; I hoped. I didn't think I would sleep as I lay listening to my son's labored breathing. *Oh, my darling,* I thought. *I'm not ready to let you go. It's not fair. You aren't even nineteen yet. God promised if we have enough faith, all things are possible, and I believed, oh, how I believed you would be cured. And what about the hundreds and hundreds of other people praying for you?*

But the doctor had said no more than two weeks at the most, and the two weeks were up. He put up a gallant fight did my long tall son these past seven months, and his poor thin body could fight no more. I was glad we had brought him home from the hospital. I dreaded the pain the doctors said he would suffer when his other lung collapsed, but he hated the hospital so much that this was the last thing we could do for him. I know Dr. Dyment approved. I could tell he loved John. He spent time with him and listened to him, and he also called almost every evening to check on him.

John made the most of these last days, seeking out his friends, going to movies and out to eat, and even attending a practice session with a rock group. How he loved rock music. His record collection was extensive. He visited as many friends as he could find. A lot of them avoided him because they couldn't bear to say good-bye to this bright laughing friend of theirs, either.

My tired body gave in, and I slept.

Six o'clock. The alarm went off. *John!* I thought immediately. But from his bed came the soft sound of his breathing. *Thank you, God,* I thought. *I'll still have time to say good-bye.*

As I packed my husband's lunch and shushed the kids as they got ready for school, I wondered if I should ask Jim and the kids to stay home, but I decided against it. Maybe I imagined that this was John's day to leave us.

About eight thirty, John became restless. "I feel so strange, Mom," he said. "I'm not taking any more of this medication."

This is it, I thought. I went to the phone to call Jim home. He came quickly and John asked, "Why are you home, Dad?"

"Because I switched oxygen tanks and wanted him to check them," I immediately answered for Jim. I still could not say a straight forward good-bye. I don't know if Jim could have, either.

Father Crumbly called that morning, and Jim told him John was dying. He came out at once.

"Why are you here, Father?" John asked.

"I told you I'd be out Friday morning to give you Communion," Father Crumbly replied. Again the avoidance of saying good-bye.

After Father Crumbly gave him Communion, he sat with us for an hour or so. I know he must have thought of the magic show John had performed for him only two days before. John was a talented magician. Those long slender hands of his could baffle everyone. They also played the piano with great feeling, and a pencil or pen in those hands produced creative works of art. Too much talent here for us to say good-bye to.

At one point, John sat up and looked at Father Crumbly. "Why Father? I have prayed so hard. Why doesn't God hear me?"

"He hears you," Father Crumbly replied.

I stood beside John all that day holding his hand and crying. Jim wept, too. John dozed off and on and restlessly kicked and threw his covers off. "What's in that corner?" he asked once.

"Your white dove," I replied. It was the white dove I'd given him for his magic tricks.

"Oh," he said. But later I was to wonder if it was the dove he saw or the spirits coming for him.

"Would you fix me a cup of coffee, Suzanne?" I asked my sister who had been staying with us these past few weeks. I was reluctant to leave him for even a moment.

John said, "I would like one, too." As John sipped his coffee, he stared at the TV. The TV Jim had been staring at without seeing since he came home. That hypnotic, mind numbing eye that is in every hospital or doctor's office, the opiate meant to ease the fear or pain of those who suffer. Was it working for John? It wasn't for me.

The afternoon wore on with him dozing restlessly. At one time, he sat up, looked at Jim and said, "Thank you, Dad, for being here." About two o'clock, he sat up again and stared off into the corner with a puzzled look on his face. Finally, he gave a nod of acknowledgement and said simply, "God." With that, he lay back into my arms, and I held this first born child of mine against my breast while he slept. I felt and listened to his soft breathing feeling the nearness of death. I listened for each breath, the silences, and then another breath. Again and again each time slower. We had almost come full cycle from birth to death. Soon he would leave me, and I still hadn't said good-bye.

At five 'til three, the door banged open as the kids came home from school; Joey, Susan and Mary with healthy exuberance. They stopped abruptly as they took in the scene in the family room.

"Is he dying?" Joey asked.

"Yes," I answered. With that all three of them ran from the room sobbing.

In a few minutes, Joey came back. "How soon?" he asked.

I looked down at my child. His chest was still. "He's gone," I replied. My heart cried out. "Good-bye my darling, John. Good-bye." As I held him tightly, surely he finally heard me.

John died at three o'clock on a Friday afternoon. That was God's way of telling me that John was in Heaven with Jesus, and it was not a final good-bye.

<><><><><><><>

After John died, I went to college and became an elementary teacher. While teaching, I got a Master's Degree in English. I retired from teaching a few years ago to have time to write. Currently I'm working on a memoir, *Letters to John*.

Every year for the anniversary of my son's death, October 3, 1980, I write a poem and put it in the local newspaper along with his picture. And every year I worry about what I can come up with that's new or different, but somehow something always comes to me shortly before that time. Sometimes I wonder if John has some hand in helping me write the poems I write for him. I'd like to believe that. The following was written after my son, Joe, tore off the roof over an attic area to expand the second floor up into two new rooms including an upstairs bathroom.

Magic Memories
By Gloria Alden

Off came the roof exposing artifacts
of my life and yours.
From under the eaves
I dug them out one by one,
memories wrapped in cobwebs
softened by the dust of years.
I dusted off your magic tricks
and carefully repacked them
still refusing to examine
the secrets they held.
As the patter from your last show
echoed in my ears,
with love I refolded your tux
tucking in brightly colored scarves
and your card - John A - Magician.
The roof has been replaced,
your magic tricks boxed
and stored once more.
Those boxes hold memories,
hidden gifts stored away,
but they cannot hold
the magic of you.

My Brother Jerry and I
By Gloria Alden

My brother Jerry and I were the only siblings for almost six years before three sisters came along and then a baby brother when I was almost twenty-one and married. Jerry was sixteen months younger than me, and in those early years I watched over him. That is until he became an annoying pest.

One of the annoying things he did to torment me was to repeat everything I said always with that impish look in his vivid blue eyes. I should have just shut up and not said anything, but I didn't. Finally, I realized if I started whistling; he had to stop because he couldn't whistle – at least not when we were kids. Maybe he never did learn that skill.   We both took piano lessons when we were young, but my brother started a year before I did. I don't remember why, but when I finally started, he was doing quite well. I'd work laboriously at those simple tunes like "Twinkle, Twinkle Little Star", and when I'd leave the piano, he'd sit down and play the same tunes adding trills and other rifts to make it beautiful. He had a natural talent on the piano that continued all his life, but at that time all it did was annoy me. After a year of piano lessons in which I didn't improve much, my parents asked if I'd rather have piano lessons or a bicycle. I chose a bicycle, so that ended the piano lessons. I never did get a bike. My brother continued with the lessons until the teacher said he'd advanced beyond her abilities to teach him anything more. Since such a teacher wouldn't be within walking distance like this one, all lessons stopped and from then on he was self-taught and became a talented pianist. I remember winter days curled up in a chair reading, while he was playing songs like "The Flight of the Bumblebee" which even on the old upright piano in the basement was beautiful. Eventually, after he married, he bought a baby grand and then his music soared even more.

In those early days, we lived next to our grandparents' farm which was on both sides of the road. Our home was on one side, and two of our cousins lived across the road from us. Norman was a year older than I was and Dolores a year younger. The four of us, and sometimes other cousins who lived rather close spent our springs catching pollywogs, our winters sliding down a hill beside the farm house and summers playing in the barn or other outbuildings and roaming the fields and woods. Sometimes we hiked to a deeper area of the creek that ran through the farm and beyond that was under a train trestle to swim, but when I discovered leeches on my leg that ended that.

Once the four of us built a clubhouse with scrap wood we found around the farm. The boys did the cutting and nailing while Dolores and I helped find boards and held them in place. When it was finished, we somehow got it balanced on a little red wagon and hauled it across the road, down a farm lane that bordered corn fields back to the woods and settled it there. The four of us barely fit in that clubhouse, and it was not high enough for us to stand up in, either.

Dolores and I loved Roy Rogers, and we had a picture of him we shared. We decided our club house needed some sort of decoration, so we put his picture on one of the walls. We were horrified and furious when we came back the next day and found out one of our brothers had drawn a black mustache and beard on our hero. I think it was Jerry; he was the most creative of the two.

There were three grandsons, but our grandpa favored Jerry over the other two. He'd take my brother fishing with our grandma. He'd also take him to visit his friends, and they all were fond of him, too. Grandpa took the two of us to country fairs, but not the other cousins. Not only was Jerry a hard worker whenever Grandpa needed help, but when he set up a stand to sell the sweet corn he raised, of the three boys who took turns minding the stand, Jerry was the only one who never helped himself to money in the cash box, unlike the other two. My brother, as well as the rest of my family, was always honest. We couldn't imagine being anything else. Well, maybe not telling all we should tell if it would get us into trouble, at least in my case, but only fudging a little and avoiding some details.

Jerry was frugal. He saved the money he earned on the farm and bought an old Model T or Model A Ford that didn't run. He had it hauled home and worked on it until it ran. He wasn't old enough to have a driver's license, so he tore around the farm paths or through uncultivated fields like a NASCAR driver with the car full of cousins and me. Those who didn't fit inside rode on the running board hanging on for dear life as he sped around sometimes in tight circles. Once a cousin fell off, and the back wheel ran over her foot. Why there were no broken bones in her foot; I have no idea.

When I was fifteen, I had a boyfriend of sorts. I wasn't allowed to date, and the guy wasn't old enough to drive, but he'd ride his bike to my place. One summer afternoon we were sitting on the back steps talking, and my brother locked the screen door. Then he pretended to read from my diary, which was a three-ring notebook and quite thick. Not only did he pretend to read, he made up things about how I loved kissing Tom, etc. etc. Things I never wrote in there. I jumped up screaming at him and pounded on the door yelling for my mother to stop him. Maybe she didn't hear because she was upstairs, but she never came down to check. Meanwhile, Tom was laughing and so was Jerry. I could have killed him that day. Well, not literally.

One day when I was working, Jerry took his canoe and my two younger sisters, Elaine and Suzanne, out to Mosquito Lake. There he launched the canoe with them sitting in the front and middle with paddles. He was in the back with a small outboard motor attached to one side. The girls paddled out onto the lake, and when a motor boat passed them going rather slow, Jerry started his motor and the girls started paddling as hard as they could until with the canoe's motor on the side away from the boat they passed, it looked as if the girls were paddling faster than the motor boat they'd just passed. I wish I could have seen the looks of amazement on the people in the boats they passed that day.

Jerry never lost his sense of humor and his playful nature, but it was never cruel. He never ridiculed people or deliberately hurt anyone. He was always a hard worker and honest. He quit college in his senior year because he ran out of money. A wealthy friend of Grandpa's, George Jones, wanted to pay for Jerry's last year, and he said no. Then a friend offered it as a loan, and Jerry still said no. In later years, he thought maybe he should have agreed to the loan. George Jones did leave Jerry a car in his will.

Eventually, after several jobs, Jerry became an iron worker. It seems a strange job for a highly intelligent person, who was an avid reader of scientific journals and other non-fiction books as well as TIME magazine and several newspapers, but it paid well, and it helped him support his family and realize their dreams.

After college Jerry, met and eventually married Joanne. After their first daughter was born, they bought a large farm in the country with a beautiful setting. The only problem was the house was built in 1842 and had no indoor plumbing. One of our uncles gave Jerry a pack of matches and told him to burn it down and to build a new house. But it was something neither Jerry nor Joanne ever considered. They moved a trailer onto the farm, put in a septic system, and lived there for several years while Jerry while working his job, also worked to restore the house by installing plumbing and updating the electrical wiring and other things while still keeping the character of the more than century old farmhouse. Over the years, he added on creating new beautiful rooms all tastefully decorated by his wife, who has a real talent in decorating.

Meanwhile, he also added a row of assorted evergreens down the long drive that led from the country road to the house. They were ones he'd started as seedling on our grandparents' farm when he was still a teenager. He planted and propagated thousands of hostas around his place, and planted over a thousand white pine seedlings that were to be the money to send his daughters, Maria and Amanda, to college. He also planted hundreds of rhododendrons. Once a neighbor took some pictures of the inside of the house and outside and sent them to *Country Living* magazine. They contacted Jerry and Joanne and wanted to feature their home in the magazine. Jerry refused. He didn't want their privacy invaded by sightseers.

And still his sense of humor and playfulness continued. Once he had Joanne drop him off at the school before classes let out. He boarded Amanda's school bus and sat there in the front seat where she'd notice him as soon as she got on. Since she was a young teenager then, she was mortified as he rode all the way to their stop.

Whenever, someone stopped to visit, he'd always ask if they'd like a piece of fudge. Of course, almost everyone would say yes – who doesn't like chocolate? Well maybe a few don't. He'd then
say, "I would, too. I wish we had some." It became an old joke, so we all went along with it. He wasn't becoming forgetful. It was just something that still made us laugh because it was so Jerry.

Joanne was very sociable and made friends wherever she went. Although Jerry would talk with ease with anyone he met and made friends, he preferred staying home on the farm or visiting with family. He loved when we had sibling nights once a month with a meal followed by playing cards, a movie or just talking. He loved his wife, daughters, and grandchildren. No husband, father or grandfather, could have been more devoted.

And he never stopped dreaming of plans for the farm he loved. He added on to the house creating a master bedroom with a sitting room and a large window looking out over his farm that anyone would love to have. He added a sun porch that had windows on two sides also with views of his beautiful farm. It was where we ate in the summer time. For his grandchildren, he built a fantastic three story playhouse/fort. He also built a bridge across the creek in the gully by the driveway and a lattice building where he propagated hostas, ferns and other plants. He built things for his siblings and daughters for Christmas gifts, too. One was a large pyramid tower for roses and clematis to grow on. Another time he hollowed out large old stones once used as building blocks for buildings to make planters. He also made glass terrariums shaped like a building for all of us.

After his first bout of cancer, he slowed a little, but not much. His next bout of cancer, this time in his lungs about eight years later slowed him a lot. He still worked outside in his extensive gardens, but because he needed to stop and rest often, he placed benches or chairs throughout his gardens and landscaped areas. He didn't survive his third bout which came years later. But up until the last cancer claimed him, he still had plans of what he wanted to do. He still read and played the piano exquisitely. My sister-in-law cherished those stubby working hands that could still create such beautiful music. And he never lost his sense of humor.

He died shortly before Christmas and per agreement with a local medical college; his body was donated to the college. Joanne held a memorial service for Jerry at a restaurant in Warren, Ohio, where her one daughter lived, and Joanne stayed while Jerry was in a hospital there. Although it was only three days before Christmas and the weather was snowy, over two hundred and fifty people showed up coming from where they lived almost fifty miles away and even as far as Columbus, Ohio and other places. There would have been even more if Joanne had contacted the Iron Workers Union Hall, because according to several who heard about it and came, they all really liked Jerry. There were many people who stood up and paid tribute to him that day. One of the things I remember was something our cousin Jeff said. He said Jerry would find out what the other person was interested in and get them to talk about it, and no matter what it was, Jerry knew enough about it to keep the conversation going, listening closely to what the other person was saying. It didn't matter if it was a young child or an older person, he listened to what that person had to say, drawing them out with questions showing his interest. I remember one of Joanne's sisters saying once that Jerry was a walking encyclopedia of useless information. We smiled about that, but in reality, is there anything such as useless information? In Jerry's case, it made him an interesting person, I think.

For the last few years, Joanne has had a celebration for Jerry on or close to his December 29th birthday with dinner at her home for their daughters, grandchildren and his siblings. It's an event filled with laughter more than tears because we tell funny

Jerry stories about the things he did that still make us laugh. Yes, we all miss him, but how lucky each and every one of us was to have had him in our lives.

The Miser and His Gold
An Aesop's Fable

Once upon a time there was a Miser who used to hide his gold at the foot of a tree in his garden; but every week he used to go and dig it up and gloat over his gains. A robber, who had noticed this, went and dug up the gold and decamped with it.

When the Miser next came to gloat over his treasures, he found nothing but the empty hole. He tore his hair, and raised such an outcry that all the neighbors came around him, and he told them how he used to come and visit his gold.

"Did you ever take any of it out?" asked one of them.

"Nay," said he, "I only came to look at it."

"Then come again and look at the hole," said a neighbor; "it will do you just as much good."

Moral of Aesops Fable: Wealth unused might as well not exist

Thoughts from Parents

Biting is not an acceptable behavior.

Toddlers might bite if they:

Lack the language skills necessary for expressing important needs or strong feelings like anger, frustration, joy, etc. Biting is a substitute for the messages he can't yet express in words like:

- I am so mad
- You are standing too close to me
- I am really excited
- I want to play
- I am experimenting to see what will happen
- I need more active playtime
- I am so tired
- My teeth hurt

What can I do to prevent biting?
Watch your child and ask who, what, when, why and where?

If you see signs that your child might be on the verge of biting, you can:

Distract your child with a toy or book. Suggest looking out the window or taking a walk to another room or outside. The goal is to reduce the tension and shift your child's attention. Sharing is one of the most common triggers for biting. Teach them to verbalize what is bothering them. For example: "Suzie, you can tell Josh:" "You are a too close to me. Leave me alone."

Read up on what to do when a child bites.

Teach him it is not acceptable. Neither is kicking or hitting another person, child or adult (unless roughhousing with an adult).

My son, if you accept my words and store up my commands within you, turning your ear to wisdom and applying your heart to understanding—indeed, if you call out for insight and cry aloud for understanding, and if you look for it as for silver and search for it as for hidden treasure, then you will understand the fear of the LORD and find the knowledge of God. (Proverbs 2:1-5)

Chapter Six

When Tommy was six years old, the teacher asked him to take some books to the library. He said, "No." She asked, "What do you mean, no? If you are afraid, I'll get Joey to go with you." He said, "If you're going to get Joey to go with me, just let him take the books." Needless to say, she didn't see any humor in his reasoning. I couldn't help but laugh; I just didn't let her see me, nor him for that matter.

Mike Staton

At age 62, Mike Staton took early retirement so he could move to Las Vegas and finish writing the third book of his fantasy trilogy *Larenia's Shadow*, an epic tale of betrayal and revenge set amid the decadent age of a long-lived empire. Books one and two, *The Emperor's Mistress* and *Thief's Coin*, have been published. The first draft of *Assassins' Lair* is one-third complete; in fact, it's been stalled at that point for several years.

That's because Mike returned to what he did early in his professional life ... reporting for a newspaper. He had been a news and sports reporter for newspapers in a small eastern North Carolina county since 2010 after working more than 20 years as a technical writer developing industrial training manuals. But after early retirement, Mike gave most of his furniture to Goodwill, then packed up his late-model Saturn and drove the nation's wondrous interstate system to Vegas where he has joined his friend Sharon and her father Charles.

Sharon, a former journalist/graphic artist who worked with Mike at a Central Florida newspaper, will be his editor, making sure his copy is spotless. Already she has helped him prepare this short story, *The Raft Trip*.

The publisher of Mike's fantasy novels is Wings ePress: http://wingsepress.com/. The books can be purchased on Amazon: http://www.amazon.com/Michael-Staton/e/B007ZSSNRM.They're also available on the Barnes & Noble website:http://www.barnesandnoble.com/w/emperors-mistress-michael-staton/1109995337?ean=2940014203524

The Rafting Trip
By Mike Staton

Eddie Slinka swept his dirt-stained hand through his sweaty brown hair and studied the cacti-dotted valley littered with sheep bones. The tall, lanky 12-year-old boy stepped toward the animal skeletons, but stopped when I didn't follow.

"What's the matter?" Eddie frowned, but then "Don't be a sissy!"

I crossed my arms against my chest and dug the tips of my P.F. Flyers into the soft sand. "Forget you, Eddie." I formed my hand into the shape of a pistol and jabbed my arm toward the graveyard of dead sheep. "Mom and dad don't want me going near the bones. Dad says this herd had tetanus and had to be killed."

He laughed. "Fraidy cat! Mike's a fraidy cat, fraidy cat, fraidy cat." Eddie ducked as I knelt, picked up a clod of dirt and hurled by his head. "Hey, stop that!"

"Dad says we shouldn't be touching the skulls. We can get the disease from them even though they're dead. Lockjaw. If you get lockjaw, you won't be able to talk. What a shame." I rolled my eyes. "For you. Me – on the other hand – will get some much needed silence."

The two rugged foothills and the valley of bones linked  upper-crust Providence Place and the prosaic Heritage Homes where Eddie's and my families were side-by-side neighbors off Hammer Road in Corona, California. It was the fall of 1965, and sixth grade had been *live* for just two weeks. The summer sun still beat down on our backs, but not like July. Instead of 105, the mid-September temperature preferred a cool 95 degrees. But almost-teenagers don't wilt under a hot California sun hovering in a nearly cloudless azure sky – not today, not in '65.

"Then stay here, crybaby," Eddie mocked, proceeding down the hill to the remains of the nearest animal.

Eddie scooped up a sun-bleached skull, and holding it away from his grimacing face as if he toted a moldy pack of baloney, he ran toward me.

"Bet you get sick," I flung back. "Bet your willy falls off."

"Not mine," he laughed, continuing his willy-nilly charge. "Yours – after I rub the skull against your nose."

 He chased me up and then down the hill toward Newhall Drive in our neighborhood. I knew I was in trouble when the sound of his tennis shoes slapping the sand overwhelmed his cackles. I felt his thick arms wrap around my waist, and then both of us rolled rest of the way down the hill, somehow not rolling over or against cacti. Straddling my waist, Eddie wiggled the skull against my cheek and chin. Furious, I pressed against the skull even as the smell of dust and creosote invaded my nose. The skull slid from Eddie's fingers, bounced on the sand, then rolled against a creosote bush.

"Eddie, you son-of-a-gun," I sputtered as he flopped beside me and giggled like a little girl at a slumber party.

"You should see your face, Mike," he said playfully. "You look like my little brother after mom tells him he has to do his homework. You're a sourpuss." Eddie tucked the skull against his side and helped me to my feet with his other hand. "I've a great idea for the skull. Let's go to stepdad's garage, OK?"

"Long as I don't have to touch the thing," I muttered, my curiosity piqued.

Eddie winked. "I'll be doing all the touching. You need to pat me on the back and say. 'You're a genius, Eddie."

Behind Eddie's house, fellow sixth-grader Cynthia Brown sunned on a chaise lounge next to the above-ground pool. The blonde adjusted her polka-dot bikini top turned onto her hip and eyed the skull nested against Eddie's belly. Her eyes grew large. "That's nasty," Cynthia shouted, her voice sour. "You won't be dancing with me anytime soon, Eddie Slinka." She turned onto her stomach and ignored us.

"Stuck-up girl!" Eddie growled under his breath, but not so softly that I couldn't hear his words. "We're not going to any stupid dance tonight anyway. I think it's time to try out the raft."

Now my eyes were growing larger. "Today? I need more time to convince mom and dad."

Eddie shook his head. "No convincing needed, Mike. Just do it. They don't need to know. When we get back, just say we went to the Little League ball field."

"I'll miss supper."

Eddie's eyebrows arched. "It won't be the first time. Grow some gonads, mister." He chuckled.

The raft, our summer project, lay propped against the garage wall near the door into the kitchen. When we weren't busy playing Little League baseball, swimming in the municipal pool or riding our 10-speeds on the neighborhood roads, we were in Eddie's backyard hoping for a glimpse of Cynthia Brown as we built the raft board by board and nail by nail. The boards and nails came courtesy of the construction crews building the next phase of Heritage Homes. In the darkness, when the sawing and hammering had ended, Eddie and I slinked among the unfinished houses, helping ourselves to what we figured we needed. Now we were nearly done. Only a few boards remained to be nailed into place.

"I know I said we'd finish up Monday afternoon," Eddie said briskly, no doubt figuring to overpower my doubts with staccato words. "But why not now? We can take it to the creek later in the afternoon. Heck with the school dance and Cynthia. Help me get it outside." He set the skull on a work table and jabbed his hand toward the garage's back door and the backyard.

To be honest, I thought we'd finish the raft, and it would never leave Eddie's garage. I should have known better since Eddie is much more adventuresome than me and is willing to deceive his mother and stepfather.

I didn't say no to Eddie's rafting trip, but neither did I say yes. Actually, I hoped he'd decide not to miss his mother's supper and put off the trip for another day.

Even with a portion of the raft's deck still unfinished, we struggled to get the raft out the back door and onto the patio between the grill and the umbrella-shaded table. It was solidly built. With a sail, it could have carried Robinson Crusoe and Friday to civilization, or so two 12-year-old experts believed.

I held the planks in place as Eddie hammered them into place. A quick glance into the Brown's yard left me distressed. Cynthia gathered up her glass of sweet tea and the suntan lotion and headed for the sliding glass door.

"I think we're bothering Cynthia," I reported dourly.

Eddie harrumphed "She doesn't care squat for you or me, Mike. Roger Gall says she and Jackie Tarr just started going steady. And anyway we won't be at the dance; we'll be floating down Goose Creek."

I'd dreamed of kissing Cynthia Brown since I first saw her helping her dad unload the U-Haul trailer at their house on Spruce Street. That she was apparently now holding hands with Jackie Tarr and getting ready to sneak kisses at tonight's dance was not good news. I really didn't want to see the spectacle.

"So how are we going to get to the Goose?" I said, handing Eddie a nail for the last plank.

"Gary..." Eddie said his big brother's name matter-of-factly, as if Gary, a high school senior, would give up his Friday hugathon with his girlfriend Sharon. I figured I stood a better chance of seeing Gary at the EUB church on Sunday morning than sitting in Gary's truck as he hauled the raft and us out to the creek.

"You're planning to give him your allowance for the next five years?" I chuckled, impressed with my wit.

"Save it!" Eddie super-glued a large block of wood to the last two planks. "Sharon's sick. He'll take us if you give him your 1955 Sandy Koufax rookie card."

Eddie screwed the sheep's skull into the block of wood, then stepped back to admire his handiwork. I concurred with his self-satisfied nod.

"Wow! That's weird. I like it," I said grudgingly.

"It's our Viking demon ship," Eddie beamed.

Demon ship. I let the words roll off my tongue. Great sound, I decided. *Now where did I put that Koufax card?*

Nowadays there's a darn, four-lane highways, lodges, restaurants and hotels. But in the early '60s only two-lane country roads, one paved, the rest gravel, took the risk-takers down to the creek bank lined with sycamores and live oaks. Eddie refused to take his pickup beyond the gravel road, and he wouldn't leave the driver's seat. Instead, he gawked at his pristine Koufax card as Eddie and I wrestled the raft down a reedy ravine to the bank.

Even with recent rains, sections of the creek weren't navigable. Instead of flowing water, the creek bed lay naked to the mid-afternoon autumn sky, sandy white as an elderly man's bald noggin. We slid the raft down the bank and watched it splash into the creek. A sudden breeze ruffled the leaves of the oaks and sycamores and tousled my hair. I took off my shirt and tied it around my waist, then waded into the water, which only reached my knees.

"I gave up Cynthia Brown for this," I complained.
Eddie shook his head sharply, sending his bangs dancing across his forehead. "No, this rafting trip saved you from a whipping from Jackie Tarr. Get that girl out of your mind, Mikie."

A fish splashed behind me, and I took a gander, but Eddie's words soon snagged my attention. "Holy cow! I can't believe how deep the water has become." Eddie squatted so that it looked like he stood in water up to his neck.

I huffed and felt my jaw tighten. "You're not being funny, Eddie."

"I really am almost over my head. Come on over to me, and you'll see."

"You can stand up, Eddie. You can't trick me."

"I am standing up." Eddie's lips curved into his *Honest Injun* smile. "It's a sinkhole. I ain't kidding."

I braced my hands on my hips and glared. "I'll join you in your damned sinkhole. And when the water doesn't rise above my kneecaps, I'm going to yank you to your feet." And yank his arms right out of their sockets, I thought, twirling my imaginary Snidely-Whiplash moustache.

"Get ready for a Jackie-Tar whipping," I hollered, taking two steps toward Eddie.

The first step went as I expected. The second step ... well, it was – as Neil Armstrong would say in 1969 – a "long run."

The water rose to my thighs – and my toes had yet to touch the sandy bottom.

Oh crap ... the water kept rising ... lapping my waist and belly button, then my chest, my neck, my chin. A weird thought sneaked into my adolescent dynamo brain: *Thank the Lord Eddie isn't Dorothy and me the Tin Man. I'd be rusting up and unable to move.*

Actually, I hate *The Wizard of Oz*. Way too much singing and except for the rat-faced flying monkey dudes, not enough action. Had I written the children's story instead of L. Frank Baum, Dorothy would be eviler than the Wicked Witch of the West, and after making the flying monkeys allies, she'd conquer Oz.

Water poured into my mouth and down into my stomach, mixing with a snack of a Hostess berry pie and a can of Coke. Still, my feet hadn't touched the river bottom. Panic deleted my Dorothy daydreams, and I began floundering in the water, arms and legs kicking wildly.

More water gushed into my nostrils, and just when I feared I might sink out of sight, my feet touched sand. When my panic— loud as a Rolling Stones song – subsided, I heard Eddie's hysterical laughter.

"You were so funny, Mike," he hooted. "You actually thought you were going to die."

I hopped up and down, trying to keep my mouth and nose above water, all the while spitting out a jet of gritty water full of sand. "OK ... you ... were ... right," I gasped between pants. "You're ... not ... squatting. But ... you ... make ... an ugly ... Dorothy."

Startlement scrawled across Eddie's face. "What in tarnation are you mumbling about?"

"Nothing. Forget it."

I hopped through the water, and when the level dropped to mid-chest I sighed as if I'd just tasted my mom's roast beef, peas and mashed potatoes. My knees brushed against the wall of sand – more a ramp – and soon I stood in thigh-level water. Eddie slashed through the water and pulled up beside me. He watched me lean over and cough up more water.

"For a second, I thought you might drink every last ounce of the Goose." Eddie slapped my back a bit harder than necessary, and a torrential stream of water exited my mouth. "Mikey, you're the champion of creek drinkers."

"I gave up my Sandy Koufax for this," I growled. "I could be dressing for the dance right about now."

Eddie shook his head derisively and said, "This is much more fun than feeling Jackie Tarr's fist flattening your nose."

"I'm not so sure," I rejoined, scowling, shifting my gaze to our raft bobbing against the bank on the other side of the sinkhole. "You're taller. It's not over your head. Go get the raft."

"Let's hear my favorite word." Eddie said, snapping his head up indignantly.

Of course, it was all for show, but I didn't want to again venture into the sinkhole. Still, I was feeling a tad obstinate. "A word? I think you mean two. Eddie's stupid."

Eddie shrugged. "I don't seem to be able to move my feet. Oh my! They're stuck in the sand."

I sighed. "You win. Please. Please get the raft."

"What did you say? I didn't quite make it out."

"Get the darn boat. Please."

Eddie plowed through the water like a Lake Arrowhead snow plow through a drift. He clambered aboard the raft and waddled to the center when starboard side tilted beneath the surface. On his knees, Eddie glowered at the skull figurehead. "Forgot the stupid paddles."

"Paddle with your hands."

"Stupid, stupid, stupid." Eddie's face held despair, as if he'd just given away *his* Sandy Koufax card. He wasn't the crying type, yet he seemed on the verge of tears.

"Our hands will work just fine. Really they will." I tried to pattern my voice like my mom's after the time I burned myself on the stove.

Eddie nodded, and gave me a rueful smile. "OK, I'll give it a try." He leaned forward until his forehead almost bumped the skull and began paddling. The raft barely moved. "It's too fraken heavy," Eddie grumbled.

I really didn't want to navigate the sinkhole. I looked up at the late-afternoon sky and thought: God, don't let me drown. "

This time I dove into the sinkhole and swam to the other side, then scrambled to my feet and joined Eddie on the raft. Our Viking demon ship tossed and turned like a real ship on stormy water as I settled in.

"Feeling seasick?" Eddie wisecracked.

"Not a teensy weensy bit," I shot back. "My family ... we're sea folk." That was a lie. The Staton and Luppenlatz men ran train depots.

Our paddling barely managed to propel the raft partway into the sinkhole, and we both were exhausted. And even if we could pick up the pace, the Goose was dry as the Sahara Desert just 50 yards ahead. We'd need to lug the monstrously heavy raft to the

next wet section. Asking Cynthia to dance and risking a beat-down by Jackie Tarr seemed more inviting than cruising down the Goose on our way-too-heavy raft.

Eddie paused his paddling and wheeled to say something to me. Eyes lifeless, expression strained, he snorted, "This stopped being –"

As if on ice, Eddie's knees slid to the starboard side, and half the raft slipped underwater. I felt myself gliding toward the edge ... faster and faster. Suddenly, I splashed into the water and saw the sky through a soggy prism. When my feet touched sand, I kicked upward and broke the surface and began a second round of hopping up and down to keep my mouth and nose out of the water.

In front of me, the raft's bow and its skull slanted upward almost 180 degrees, then slipped beneath the surface, leaving foaming bubbles that soon vanished.

Eddie strung together 10 curse words. Unexpectedly calm, he said, "Let's go home."

I nodded. "Something ... we can ... agree on."

I made my way to shallow water, climbed the bank and propped my hand against a sycamore. "I think we should have gone to the school library and checked out a book on building rafts."

"Live and learn," Eddie said lazily. "Too bad about the skull, though."

"Yea, too bad." I decided to keep sarcasm out of my voice. It'd been a rough day for Eddie – and me.

We hiked to the gravel road and stuck out our hands, hoping to hitchhike back to our neighborhood. Soon a late '40s Ford

pickup truck appeared in a dust cloud, rounding a curve that snaked around a foothill speckled with desert scrub brush. As the truck drew closer, we heard chickens squawking above the sputter and rumble of the ancient engine. Most of the truck bed consisted of wire cages filled with Rhode Island chickens.

The truck kicked up pebbles as it clattered to a stop. Inside the cab, three kids snuggled between a Mexican farmer in a bright green and red shirt and his plump esposa.

The driver stuck his head through the open window. "Afternoon, niños. Can I drop you off somewhere?"

"Si, you sure can, señor," Eddie said amicably.

"Corner of Parkridge and Corona avenues, señor," I inserted. "We can't thank you enough for lending us a hand."

As the three kids, two boys and a girl, all under five, leaned across their papá, he grinned and said, "No problema, niños. Hop in the back. Don't mind the el pollos."

We climbed over the gate and settled into a corner of the bed free of the cages. The driver revved up his noisy engine and the truck shook and rattled its way along the gravel road. Feathers flew as the pickup rolled roughly over a rut, and a few settled on my head, chest and nose.

I flicked off the one on my nose and examined the early-evening sky. The reddening sun hung above the foothills. "Looks like I'll still have time to take a bath and go to the dance."

Eddie nodded, apparently too weary to make another joke about Jackie Tarr.

"I think I'll dance only with Laura Wagner this time around," I said thoughtfully.

Eddie offered me a wicked grin. "We left our shirts."

"I think mine came off when the raft capsized," I reflected.

Eddie scratched his chin. "My mom's very understanding. Your mom ... she's not as understanding. You'd better come up with a good explanation. I won't have any fun if you're grounded for a week."

My heart rattled in my chest. "Uh oh."

The Old Hound
An Aesop's Fable

A Hound, who in the days of his youth and strength had never yielded to any beast of the forest, encountered in his old age a boar in the chase. He seized him boldly by the ear, but could not retain his hold because of the decay of his teeth, so that the boar escaped.

His master, quickly coming up, was very much disappointed, and fiercely abused the dog.

The Hound looked up and said: "It was not my fault, master; my spirit was as good as ever, but I could not help mine infirmities. I rather deserve to be praised for what I have been, than to be blamed for what I am."

Moral of Aesops Fable: No one should be blamed for his infirmities.

Thoughts from Parents

There is no one like your boy.

Children develop through a sequence of steps and milestones; they may not proceed through these steps in the same way or at the same time. The boy's attention spans are growing, and they want to try new experiences.

Children this age (6 or so) write stories, notes and descriptions. Most are able to develop an idea beyond a sentence and will add some details to help describe or explain things in their world. They enjoy sharing their writing with others.

Make believe and reality are a little blurred. They may have an imaginary friend, or feel that their toys are their friends. They may give animals human characteristics, such as suggesting what a worm might be thinking, or that a butterfly has eye lashes. Gentle encouragement to look closely at worms and butterflies will help children to describe more objectively what they observe.

Young boys enjoy moving in a variety of ways. Although far from proficient in motor skills, this does little to dampen their enthusiasm for trying out new activities and sports. They are able to run in various pathways and directions and can manipulate their bodies by jumping and landing, rolling and transferring their weight from feet to hands to feet. Their hand- and foot-eye coordination is still developing, so skills like throwing, catching, kicking and striking are still emerging.

Little guys show greater creativity and complexity in the use of props, costumes, movements and sounds. They love to dress up in oversized clothes and shoes. The best way to deal with boys of this age is to stay calm and be creative. They can be talked into almost anything, especially if you make it sound like fun.

Teach your son to make good choices at an early age.

The proverbs of Solomon: A wise son brings joy to his father, but a foolish son brings grief to his mother. (Proverbs 10:1)

Chapter Seven

At seven years old, Tommy was constantly getting hurt. I asked, "Is he lacking calcium or something? His bones seem to be so fragile." The doctor picked up the edge of my son's cast and said, "Bones can only take so much torture before they break." He smiled at me and asked the nurse to prepare the items he needed to put a new cast on Tommy's arm. The doctor said, "Young man, take it easy on those bones." With a wink, he said, "Mom don't worry so much, boys will be boys." ~Cher'ley

Linda McKeel Scott

Linda Scott lives in Hartselle, Al. with her husband Stephen. She has two grown sons, three grandsons and one granddaughter. She and her husband are retired truckers. They are enjoying their retirement with their three rescue animals, Lexie the Italian Greyhound, Redley the Min Pin, and Earl, the biggest domestic cat ever.

McKeel is not a common name, so she's happy to see it in print. She enjoyed writing the stories about her sons and hope you all enjoy them as well.

End of Story
By Linda McKeel Scott

My family lived in Colorado Springs, Colorado for about 6 years. We discovered this delightful park, Palmer Park, that was a smaller version of the "Garden of the Gods", which is a registered National Natural Landmark, with dramatic views, 300' towering sandstone rock formations. On the weekends, we loved going to Palmer Park for cook outs, and it was a fun place to spend time and get close to nature, the rock formations were quite beautiful and it boasted picnic areas with grills and tables along with jogging trails as well as the red rocks and climbing areas. The Gods was for tourists; Palmer Park was for the locals and we loved it.

My husband, our two sons Stephen IV-8 and Ken-6, my husband's brother John and future sister-in-law Penny were enjoying the day. Penny and I were grilling steaks and getting the table set up when I realized the boys were gone. I got a horrible feeling in the pit of my stomach. From our picnic table, we had a clear view of the cliffs where people climbed. The boys

had been there before but never without their dad to keep an eye on them. From deep inside my gut, I felt something was not right. I looked around and spotted them climbing up that cliff. Fear gripped my heart. I started screaming. It was a good distance away, and my husband sped towards the cliffs.

I crammed my fist in my mouth to try to calm my panic. I saw Ken, our youngest, slipping. He had lost his grip, and he was going to fall to his death. His dad and I were too far away to help him.

His older brother who was above him looked down and recognized Ken's dilemma. He assessed the situation, scrambled down until he was on a ledge below his younger brother. Ken would have bypassed the ledge on his way to the rocky ground below. Stephen managed to push him back up to the safety of a small ridge that would hold him until someone else could get to him.

My sons were close in age and very competitive and always said they hated each other. So when all was done, and the terror of the moment subsided, I said to my oldest son, "For a kid who claims to hate his brother, you sure acted quickly."

He calmly replied, "It is not in my nature to watch someone fall to their death. End of story." He actually said end of story.

Coulrophobia and a Good Beating
By Linda McKeel Scott

The boys are 14 and 16, and we are living in Alabama. My oldest son Steve had a great fear of clowns, which I thought was kind of funny, since clowns make people laugh at the circus and at kids' birthday parties. However, I found out it is not an uncommon occurrence among many people to think of clowns as sinister, and frightening. Coulrophobia is a real fear and causes a feeling of terror in those who are afraid of clowns. Steve is among the people who are terrified of Clowns. He never made a secret of the fact, but it was never a main topic of conversation over the dinner table. However, he mentioned it a couple of times. So when he told us he was reading the Stephen King book, "It", which is about a clown, Pennywise, who terrified children, it became useful information for his brother.

My younger son, Ken, had become a very sly and clever prankster. I have to say, diabolical at times. Their competitive nature was in full swing and all the above information set up the perfect storm for Ken to spring into action.

We had all gone to bed for the evening. Steve, an avid reader, would get into bed and read some of his book until he got sleepy. When he got up to use the restroom one last time, Ken snuck into his closet, leaving it open just a crack so he could see him. We lived in an older house that had a small, cramped closet. Benjamin Franklin said, "He who can have patience can have what he will." I think Mr. Franklin had Ken in mind, because it took a lot of patience to pull off this prank. I can just imagine Ken constraining his laughter.

Steve got back into bed and continued reading his book. Ken waited about ten minutes and then ever so slightly jingled the wire hangers. He saw Steve pause from reading. He cocked his head in order to hear better; the quizzical look turned back into relaxed facial features. He shook his head, dismissed the thought of hearing something, and continued to read.

Ken waited.

Another ten minutes or so passed before he jingled the hangers again, this time, just a little more. Steve looked alarmed, pulled his book to his chest and looked around. After a few seconds, he decided it had been his imagination. The book was getting to him. He listened, looked around the room, just in case he'd missed something, satisfied that he was alone and safe, he started reading again.

Ken waited.

The cramps in his body were making it hard to stay put. Ready for his big finale, he jingled the hangers very loudly and watched Steve jump out of bed totally freaked out. The older boy very slowly made his way to the closet and gingerly opened the door. Ken stood there with a flashlight under his chin, with the most menacing look on his face that he could muster.

Just as in the Christmas poem "'Twas the Night Before Christmas", there rose such a clatter; we sprang from our beds to see what was the matter, and what to our wandering eyes should appear, but our oldest son naked straddled his brother, yelling, screaming and beating the younger one, who was laughing hysterically.

What we witnessed was disturbing. Not that they were flailing around on the floor, and beating on each other, but that we didn't know until that moment that Steve slept in the buff. . My husband and I just looked at each other, closed the door and went back to bed. I wish I could say this was an unusual day in our family, but actually, it was a day in the life of raising two boys.

"He who can have patience can have what he will."— Benjamin Franklin

The Hare and the Hound
An Aesop's Fable

A Hound having started a Hare from his form, after a long run, gave up the chase.
A Goat-herder, seeing him stop, mocked him, saying:
"The little one is the best runner of the two."
The hound replied; "You do not see the difference between us; I was only running for a dinner, but he for his life."

Moral of Aesops Fable: Incentive spurs effort.

Thoughts from Parents

Time to play outside. Learning to ride a bike, swim, ski, dance or gymnastics. They will grow very proficient with practice.

Sedentary children will not mature as quickly as those who participate in activities like dance lessons, team sports or backyard play. Young boys (even if for a half a year) who learn dance will do better in sports later in life.

This is a good time to introduce creative arts such as art, music, dance and theater. Given exposure and practice, seven-year-olds create art that depict objects more realistically and that reflect personal culture and experiences.

The discipline of practicing and the accomplishment that the young boys feel is great for their self-esteem. They respond to the mood of music through movement and dance. Boys love funny, silly songs.

Walk with your boys. Give them your full attention. Leave your cell phones at home when you are going to play with or walk with your son.

Dramatic play and puppet shows are a great way to reach young boys. Reading to your youngster is always a great time for questions and answers.

Tuck them in and pray with them at nights to make them feel secure as they sleep. Children who go to Sunday School also develop some early skills that help them in school.

Teach your sons: Honor your father and your mother, as the LORD your God has commanded you, so that you may live long and that it may go well with you in the land the LORD your God is giving you. (Deuteronomy 5:16)

. Chapter Eight

At eight years old Tommy was starting to have a lot of frustration in his life. He wanted to spread his wings farther than we wanted him to and we'd often have a power struggle. We held onto our steadfast and consistent rules, and he came around (for a while, this happened more than once). He loved animals and had several: skunks, ducks, cockatiels, rabbits, cats, dogs, and lizards. He liked to collect things like skeletons and bugs. He enjoyed the ocean and learned to swim on a cruise ship. Eight was an up and down year.

Misty Montega

An avid volunteer and musician. She is a loving mother of three children—a boy and two girls, and a devoted wife.

Misty has worked with a lot of children over the years and teaches middle-grade Sunday school classes at her church.

She wrote this story to let people who may be having problems with their child know that they are not alone. Her second story is about her true experience with a dear, sweet family. She feels some redemption from aiding them.

Raising 'em Right—Don't make 'em Right
By Misty Montega

My son is irresponsible, and he robbed a store using a gun. Am I and his father to blame? He is 38 years-old and doing time in the prison on a gun charge.

Someone could have been killed. I feel bad. Not only did I fail as a parent, but my friends look at me differently. We are victims, too. I hurt terribly that my son would even think to do something like he did.

I wonder what I might have done to change things. I have two other children who are well balanced and productive. We an average to above average life. The kids did not want for anything, but I did not give them everything they wanted. I gave him a good home.

He tries to blame me for his problems. He says I do more for the other kids. Time and again, I have gone to his aid. He skimmed through high school, got married and had a son of his own by the time he was 19. He couldn't find a decent job. We helped him as much as we could, but it was never enough. A year later he was divorced. His ex-wife only wanted him out of her life and the life of little Roger. We agreed to let him move back in with us and to help him with child support until he could get back on his feet. We paid the child support, but we weren't permitted to see our grandson, she moved away, and every time we asked to see the baby she had an excuse, like she was going out of town for some reason. The ex-wife remarried, and the new man wanted to adopt little Roger. We begged our son not to sign over his parental rights, but he signed the adoption papers anyway.

We talked him into taking some classes, and he decided he wanted to be a CPA. I don't know how long it had been since the time he quit school, and the time that we found out he'd quit. He'd used the money to buy drugs and alcohol. He added a girlfriend to our family. He got mad and moved out when we wouldn't let her stay.

Several months later he was home again, crying and begging. Promising to change.

His dad had pretty much washed his hands of him after the college classes, so in order to help him, I had to sneak around. I felt so guilty, but what's a mother to do. I gave him a little money and food, when he stopped in. He said he was really serious about changing his life.

I talked my husband into letting him move back home. He got a few jobs and moved in and out of our home, but nothing really changed. Then he got old enough that he settled down enough to go to college. We allowed him to stay with us for free. All he had to do was to get a part-time job to keep his car going, to buy insurance, and to keep everything legal on it. His car got impounded for no tags, and no insurance, plus he had pot on him when he got stopped.

He drove my car back and forth to college. I was so proud when he got a business degree.

He got messed up with the wrong crowd, and ended up robbing the convenience store, using a gun.

It was in the middle of the night that we got the call. I couldn't take anymore. I was screaming and crying in agony. I couldn't believe it, what if he'd killed someone?

I know this much; you can do everything right, and your child can still grow up and have serious problems as an adult. I never sought help, because there was never a sign of any abnormalities. He did well in school, had some friends, was in sports, and he was the sweetest boy.

Right now I am dreading his discharge. His time will be up soon. He promises me; he's changed. His dad will not talk to him right now.

Kicked to the Curb
By Misty Montega

It was a cold January morning when we picked up Michael and his sisters for Sunday school. He was in a full body cast laying on the sidewalk. His private area was exposed, and he wore no coat. He was five years old and barely spoke. His sisters weren't dressed much better; their faded dresses covered by thin jackets, which barely kept the wind off. His hair had been shorn, a blessing when you looked at his sisters matted tresses. But smiles lit up all three faces when they saw us pulling up to the curb.

We stopped at McDonald's on the way to church. Afraid that someone would think these children belonged to us; we just ordered through the drive-in window. We didn't know whether to feed them first or to clothe them first. My husband and I lived on a meager budget, with two children in college, and the third elsewhere. We decided to fill their bellies first.

I checked my watch. Just enough time to run by our house to get them dressed. This was the second week we had dressed them. Last week, I had bought things from home.

It had been three weeks since I first saw Michael laying out in the middle of his yard. I stopped to see what was going on. As soon as I stopped a woman ran down off the porch and eyed me. She bent down and put her arm around the child's shoulder, as if to protect him from me.

I said, "Hi, I'm Misty, and I'm from the First Baptist Church. Do you attend church anywhere?"

"Nope, and we don't want to. God ain't done nothin' for us."

"We have a great Sunday school program. I'd be happy to come by and pick up your son."

"I done said no."

About that time, two little girls came running up. They stood behind their mama and watched me carefully. One of them whispered something that I couldn't hear.

"Church, wants Michael."

"The oldest little girl stuck out her chest and said, "You can't have him. He's our baby brother, and we waited a long time to get him."

I knelt down. "I don't want to keep him. I would like to come by on Sunday and take him to Sunday school. I'd like to take you too, if your mama would let you go."

The mother cocked her head sideways, "How long would you be keeping 'em."

"From around 9 until noon. Sunday school starts at 10:00 and Children's church at 11:00. We always stop at McDonalds on the way to church for coffee and an Egg McMuffin."

"Please mamma, please." The three begged in near unison.

"My husband and I will be by at 9:00 next Sunday if that would be okay with you."

"Okay.." She turned to go back up the walkway. "Girls get your brother."

I returned to my car and sat inside watching as the two little girls pulled and tugged on their brother. Finally when they got him to the steps, the mother came and helped them get him the rest of the way up.

My heart was wrenched that day. How could a mother neglect her children so badly? I had not always had it easy, but I had always loved and cared for my children. They were clean and fed well. These poor babies were not. I told my husband what I had seen.

The rest of the week I went through clothes and things that we had packed away. I'd been meaning on getting rid of a lot of it anyway, but had put it off, there wasn't much that would work on those little ones. I didn't know if the children had good clothes for school, or if all they had was what they were wearing. I gathered a couple of coats that had been my daughters and some swimming trunks that had belonged to my son and one of his old school coats. Just for emergency. If they were dressed nicely, with coats then I'd leave the items I'd gathered in the car, but I had a feeling that would not be the case.

When we arrived Sunday, the children weren't out front. I went up to knock on the door. The oldest came out and in a hushed voice said, "Mamma said to go with you, but to not wake her up. Just wait in the car."

I went back to the car, and a few minutes later the two little girls emerged from the house with Michael in tow. His little feet hit the threshold of the door, and then slammed the concert porch. Before I could gasp, my husband had run up the sidewalk. He hadn't even bothered to close his car door.

Dressed the same as they were the week before, they were happy for the warm clothes I offered them. We didn't have shoes for them. The girls had on shoes, but the littlest one kicked hers off. Her little toes were so red and cramped. Neither of them had on socks and Michael had nothing on his feet. When we arrived at church there was some quizzical looks, but no one said anything. I kept all three children in my class that Sunday and I helped out with Children's Church.

I wished I had money just to go buy things for these poor babies, but I didn't. Our treat to each other was stopping at McDonald's on Sunday morning, but neither of us got anything to eat that morning and we split one coffee so we could feed the little ones.

We had a tape measure, and I wrote down all the kids' sizes. I'd make a trip to The Salvation Army and buy them what I could this week.

I tried to talk to the mother when I took the kids home, but she wouldn't come out of the bedroom. "Okay, I'll be by next Sunday to get them."

She grunted.

**

That night I went over my checking account register and my bills to see what I could move around. I found a little squeeze area.

Excitement filled me, as I took my checkbook into The Salvation Army Thrift Store. I knew I wouldn't be able to buy much, but I'd be able to get them something. When I pulled out my tape measure, I felt the need to explain to the cashier what I was doing.

She said she could help me out, go ahead and shop while she made a phone call. I felt like an elf on Christmas Eve.

Cautiously, I stayed within my budget, just in case the clerk couldn't come through, but I'd found some nice heavy coats that were marked down, and a dress for each girl. I couldn't find boots, but I found a pair of dress shoes for the oldest girl and a pair of tennis shoes for the younger one and a pair of tennis shoes for Michael. I would have to buy men's clothes for Michael so they'd fit over his cast. I even found a toboggan for him. I wanted to get the girls some pants and shirts, but they had already told me they had to wear dresses to church.

The woman who ran the register came bouncing towards me. She was smiling from ear to ear. "Get whatever you need!"

Even though the items weren't for me, I felt a little embarrassed. It's hard to receive help. That little embarrassment helped me to understand how Michael's mamma may respond. I'd have to approach her with empathy. After all, I didn't know anything about her.

Some of the women at church had suggested I call the authorities. Maybe child welfare. I'd thought about it, but the girls talked and talked about how much they loved their mamma and how good she was to them. When I looked around their neighborhood, their circumstances didn't seem much different from the others in that area. Maybe I could just get close to the mother and help her figure her life out.

Things didn't get better in leaps and bounds, but I was in contact with the school. They were healthy and made decent grades. Mamma didn't come to church regularly, but she would come by when the kids had something special going on.

Michael got his cast off. They never found out who ran over Michael, but some of the neighbors said it was Mamma's boyfriend, and that he was Michael's daddy. It was an accident. The person who ran over him, also backed back over him, which caused multiple injuries. I was in their lives up until my husband's plant closed down, and we had to move.

The oldest girl dropped out of high school, but later got a GED and went into a nursing program. The younger girl went to Cosmetology school, got married and has a little girl of her own.

Michael, well—his mamma and I are trying to talk him into going to college. He's really smart, and he could easily get a scholarship, but he won't commit. No matter what he does, he'll do well at it. He's a hard worker, and he wants all the good things life has to offer.

I'm glad that I didn't just call the authorities that day and brush off this family. It would have been devastating for the children; they may have been split up, or ended up being shifted from family to family. The way it worked out I was able to help the children and the mother too. She truly did try, but she didn't have the education or the training to go very far. Her mother had died when she was young.

To you, happy family, I say...Reach Out.

The Monkey and the Dolphin
An Aesops Fable

A Sailor, bound on a long voyage, took with him a Monkey to amuse him while on shipboard. As he sailed off the coast of Greece, a violent tempest arose, in which the ship was wrecked, and he, his Monkey and all the crew were obliged to swim for their lives.

A Dolphin saw the Monkey contending with the waves, and supposing him to be a man (whom he is always said to befriend), came and placed himself under him, to convey him on his back in safety to the shore. When the Dolphin arrived with his burden in sight of land not far from Athens, he demanded of the Monkey if he were an Athenian, who answered that he was, and that he was descended from one of the noblest families in that city.

The Dolphin then inquired if he knew the Piræus (the famous harbor of Athens). The Monkey, supposing that a man was meant, and being obliged to support his previous lie, answered that he knew him very well, and that he was an intimate friend, who would, no doubt, be very glad to see him. The Dolphin, indignant at these falsehoods, dipped the Monkey under the water, and drowned him.

Moral of Aesops Fable: He who once begins to tell falsehoods is obliged to tell others to make them appear true, and, sooner or later, they will get him into trouble.

Thoughts from Parents

I want to do it myself. You will hear this more and more often as your boy matures. Eight-year-olds enjoy having the opportunity to solve problems independently. When given a chance, they are very resourceful.

As boys mature they enjoy sharing their viewpoints on a variety of topics. They have a clearly developed sense of self-worth and may express frustration in response to activities that they perceive as areas of personal weakness.

This is the age where peer interactions, start to affect their lives. It is when you should pick your child's friends. Steer him towards children whose parents have the same goals in mind for their children as you do.

 Boys will seek out which sports or activities they want to pursue. He could be more creative depending on the arts he has been exposed to such as art, music, dance and theater. Given exposure and practice, eight-year-olds create more detailed and realistic images in their artwork. Eight-year-olds are able to create a complete dance sequence and then repeat it. This is also the age where his skills have developed more in throwing, running, catching a ball, and riding a bike. All motor skills are peaking.

Around this age, the boys will begin to identify themselves as "athletic" or "non-athletic," thereby influencing their future involvement in sports and physical activity. Even if they are not sports inclined they should still remain active and be encouraged to play and run. And on the other hand make sure they are exposed to all of the arts you can and to have them read as much as possible.

This is a good age to teach boys to control their anger. Whoever is slow to anger has great understanding, but he who has a hasty temper exalts folly." (Proverbs 14:29).

Chapter Nine

Tommy became very involved in basketball and baseball. He mostly set on the bench during the games. It was hard as a parent to watch this happen, but he felt like he was part of the team and he wanted to keep playing. Sports are not always fair, often it depends on who you know or if your dad is the coach or friends with the coach. Eventually when he got coaches who didn't have kids on the teams he became very good in all sports.

This was also the year he fell madly in love with any tall girl or woman that happened to come into his life—teacher, friend of the family, 8th grader—it didn't matter as long as they were tall.

Maxwell (Max) Taylor

Max a retired history professor who loves all things America, before 1950. Franklin Delano Roosevelt (FDR) is his favorite president, and hero. Roosevelt survived polio, the great depression, and both world wars, all while tackling the race and religion problems in America.

Max does not consider himself a writer, but he was a boy, and he dealt with some difficult problems while raising sons and in the classrooms.

Girl Watcher
By Max Taylor

The way the girls filled out their sweaters was of high interest to me. That's what girls wore in 1944. Pull over sweaters, and wool skirts to school, but some of them wore trousers after school. Since I wasn't old enough to drive, I had to hang out with guys who did. I looked older than I was, so my friends were older. I liked to spend my early evenings at the record store. Girls loved the record store. I couldn't stay too late because  I had chores and my mom would explode if we weren't all home for supper. I got yelled at a lot for having the radio too loud while doing my homework.

"Be quiet." I said as I climbed the tree outside of Suzie Jones' window. The two guys with me, Mark and Jimmy, giggled like little girls. They grunted and huffed as they pushed on me. Finally, I grabbed a branch and pulled myself up. I didn't know how I'd explain the scuffs on my shoes to my parents, but I'd worry about that later.

"How will we get up? Mark push. Lift." Jim grabbed my ankle.

"Stop, you baboon. Get down. You'll get your turn." I kicked at Jim until he turned loose. It was really hard to yell at the guys when I had to be so hushed.

When I got up to the window, I saw the most glorious sight. Girls, lots of girls, dressed in their dad's pajamas or wearing a long shirt. They were dancing, hair bouncing, legs moving up and down, round and round, and arms flying. Glorious abandonment. This was a rare occasion. I leaned back against the tree to enjoy the show. I knew them all. Suzie, Betty, Linda, Sandy, and Carol. They stopped dancing, and Betty sat across from Linda and Sandy across from Carol. Suzie had some lipstick tubes. My heart raced. Most girls weren't allowed to wear lipstick, and the ones who did were not very reputable. One of my girlfriends, would wear lipstick when we were alone, she made me swear never to tell anyone. Even grown women didn't wear lipstick outside the home very often.

I sighed loudly and grabbed my chest. I nearly fell

The noise brought the gigglers to full attention. Jim yelled, "My turn."

I said, "Wait."

He got louder. "My turn."

The porch light came on, and those two took off. It was too late for me. I froze, pushed my body as tight as I could against the tree and held my breath. Mr. Jones came off the porch and looked around. I swear he looked right at me, but he turned and went back inside. I swooshed a big gasp of air. Then I saw the living room curtain move as Mrs. Jones peeked out. Oh no, she's going to send him back out. But a few minutes later, the lights went out.

I didn't have a watch, so I had no idea what time it was. The guys had abandoned me. If I jumped, I'd surely break a leg. Maybe if I could get far enough out on the limb I could hang onto the branch and drop down. The branch cracked, and I yelled, "Whoa."

The porch light came on again. I looked up and saw five faces pressed against the window, staring down at me. Mr. Jones opened the door. "I've got a shotgun, and I'm not afraid to use it."

I half crawled, half scampered away before he could get off the porch.

I felt I had escaped with my life, but I would now have to face my dad for being late to supper and for not taking care of Prince, our dog.

And then there would be school tomorrow. Would I be labeled a pervert?

I lucked out again. The girls didn't recognize me and the two with me; Jimmy and Mark were sworn to secrecy and besides they'd get in as much trouble as I would if we were caught. I'm never doing that again.

"Max, there's a pajama party at Betty's house this weekend." Mark whispered over my shoulder, and then giggled.

The Farmer and the Stork
Aesops Fable

A Stork of a very simple and trusting nature had been asked by a gay party of Cranes to visit a field that had been newly planted. But the party ended dismally with all the birds entangled in the meshes of the Farmer's net. The Stork begged the Farmer to spare him."Please let me go," he pleaded. "I belong to the Stork family who you know are honest and birds of good character. Besides, I did not know the Cranes were going to steal."
"You may be a very good bird," answered the Farmer, "but I caught you with the thieving Cranes and you will have to share the same punishment with them."

Moral of the story: You are judged by the company you keep.

Thoughts from Parents

Boys are super sensitive around this age. It is not unusual for them to cry, pout or throw a little tantrum. The best thing a parent can do is to redirect his attention. Let him know you understand and give him something to make him feel good about himself. Does he draw well, or does he enjoy puzzles, or coloring? It might be a good time to teach him something new.

Take your son on walks, go fishing, or for a car ride. Anything that will give you some alone time without distractions.

Watch for signs of problems. This is the age where some bullying starts or gets more serious. Make sure your boy is not being bullied or that he is not doing the bullying. Talk to his teachers and Sunday school teachers.

Kids should respects all adults, but all adults are not to be trusted. If you son feels uncomfortable around someone, don't force him to be around that person. Find out why he's feeling at odds around the adult in question. It could just be that he doesn't like to be kissed by Aunt Suzie or Uncle Bob is a little rough when he pats him on the back. It may be innocent, or it may not be. If you find out something inappropriate has taken place contact the authorities, and get your child counseling, or help dealing with their emotions right away, and don't stop too quickly.

Boys may lie or tell tall tales at this age. Teach them the difference between a story and a lie. They should be allowed to express themselves but at the end of a story they need to specify that is a story. "I went to school and a giant plane fell and landed on the playground." Then they could laugh and say, "This is a story." (Of course, unless it was true.)
    Sons need to know that God is with them. "Have I not commanded you? Be strong and courageous. Do not be frightened, and do not be dismayed, for the Lord your God is with you wherever you go." Joshua 1:9

Chapter Ten

When Tommy was ten years old, he soaked us all. We were at church, and they had a baptism service. It was so cold in the room where the service was being performed that the ice had to be broken on the tub. The preacher said, "I baptize you in the name of the Father, the Son, and the Holy Spirit". He then dunked Tommy under the water. When he rose he spewed water from his mouth like a fountain and then shook like a dog. So the people who didn't get hit by the spray got soaked by the shake. Cher'ley

Cher'ley Grogg

Cher'ley writes different genres. "The Journey Back--One Joy at a Time" is a devotional book she just finished. "Stamp Out Murder" is a cozy mystery and "The Secret in Grandma's Trunk is a YA novel. Cher'ley co-authored "Small Town America" and "West Virginia Memories". She is featured in, and she has many poems, short stories and articles published online and in print books. Some of her hobbies are photography, and painting fine art. She has received awards in both mediums, and she has art is in collections throughout the United States and foreign countries. She enjoys fishing, reading, walking, dancing, and long, long baths. She loves the Lord, her husband, children, grandchildren, and great grandson. She loves spending time with each of them. Tootsie, her Cairn Terrier, is a true joy.

Her very favorite thing to do is laugh. She looks for every opportunity to share in something fun and interesting. She also likes to apply different Bible verses to her life. During the publication process of her novel, the one that speaks to her the most is found in Philippians 4:8. She likes to close with that verse. 'Finally, brothers and sisters, whatever is true, whatever is noble, whatever is right, whatever is pure, whatever is lovely, whatever is admirable--if anything is excellent or praiseworthy--think about such things.'

Surrounded by Boys
by Cher'ley Grogg

You want to know about boys, I know about boys.

I came into the world with 2 older brothers, a grandpa, a dad and several uncles and male cousins. I think I was 10 when I realized there were girls in my world besides my mom, grandma, and school. I also had two younger brothers. I have one son three grandsons, and one great grandson. I was 12 when I realized there were BOYS in the world. I can tell you about boys. What did I learn from each one?

This is Mom sitting in Grandpa's car.

Grandpa on Mom's side got killed when she was 2, he owned a riverboat which carried fur trappers and the like up and down the Ohio River. His death was suspicious. **Grandpa** on the other side was a Coal Miner, a very quiet man, whom I enjoyed making smile.

Dad was the First Mate on a River Boat. In his early years, he was pretty wild, but the wildest I remember was right before he quit drinking, he sat out on the porch talking to the dogs. I think Mom had him locked out of the house. I was watching early morning cartoons when I heard him saying, "It will be okay Duke. I'm in the doghouse too. We'll stick together boy." I'm not sure how I felt about Dad's conversation with the dog, but I thought it was very strange. Dad and I used to sit up late at night, in the stillness of the dark. We just sat and enjoyed each other's company. Before he stopped smoking, he'd write my name in the air with the fire on the tip of his cigarette. Dad taught the boys to be hunters and fishermen. He taught us all how to play ball, tag, and other outside games. Dad laughed a lot. His favorite show was the Red Skelton Show.

Every year around Halloween, **boys** would go through the neighborhoods tipping outhouses. This wasn't too hard since most water closets sat on a knoll, with the back half over an embankment. (I'll let you get a mental picture of this). Grandma's outhouse was an easy target, it wasn't that far from the main road, and she was an old woman living by herself. Every year Dad built her a new outhouse or repaired the one that was tipped. He decided he was not going to let these teenagers get by with it. He loaded his shotgun with salt and perched inside Grandma's outhouse. He fell asleep. All I can say is he did not try that again the next year.

**

Teen **boys** can be destructive. Mailbox bashing replaced the outhouse tipping. It's a boy thing. Teen boys egg each other on. They work hard to impress each other. As a teen, I rode around with a group of kids. We had as many kids stuffed into the car as we could. While cruising the country roads, one of the boys yelled. "Stop!" He bounded out of the car, grabbed a plastic goose from someone's yard, then he jumped back in, and we were off to town. We crossed the river from Ohio to West Virginia. We were giddy with emotions over the minor crime that had been committed. After crossing the river, we headed straight to Jimbo's the local fast food Drive-in, where we proceeded to drive circles around. Round and round the teens would drive, revving their motors, squealing their tires, and honking their horns. Every once in a while we'd stop for a drink or sandwich, The roller skating waitresses would pop gum and chat with the boys between hopping from car to car. Frank, one of the boys in our car, climbed out onto the hood still clinging to the goose. The local cop stopped us and accused him of stealing the goose from the yard beside the restaurant. He said, "I didn't steal it from that yard; I stole it in Ohio." After questioning us all, the officer let us move on, and Frank got to keep the goose.

**

My **oldest brother**, took on the roll of the head of the house when Dad was working, (being a first mate on the river boat, Dad had to be away from home for long periods of time). Since he was only 9 years older than me, I bulked. But, still I listened to him and respected him. He was a good mechanic, and wanted me to know how to do at least basic things to a car. I think he finally gave up. He tried to teach me to milk a cow too, but that didn't work out so well either. I was 12 when he married; his in-laws had a farm. I loved their horses. One day I jumped the electric fence and didn't make it all the way over. I was straddle the fence and my legs were bouncing back and forth, every time I tried to move, zap. I started screaming, and no one seemed to hear me. I looked toward the barn, and there Bill stood, laughing like a hyena. Finally, he turned off the power, and I was able to cross the fence. I was so mad; I didn't even look back at him.

John, my **next to oldest brother,** was easy going. Tall and quiet. He built a treehouse that we all played in, and turned a bike into a moped using an old motor of some kind. I got his hand me down bike. It was very big (I was 10). My uncle Chuck (another big-boy) put me on the bike and pushed me over a gradual downhill slope. I learned to ride the first time I was on it because as the hill progressed, it turned into an embankment. The thing I remember the most about John was after he got home from the service I was a young teen, and wasn't allowed to date by myself. I got the bright idea of going on a double date with John. We went to the Drive-in theatre. I sat in the backseat and watched him snuggle with his honey in the front seat, so I did a little smooching of my own. John never said a word. When we got home, he was talking to Mom. He got louder and louder. His face was red, and he was jabbing the table with his finger (to make his point). I heard him say, "Never again. I will not go on a double date with her. All I could do was keep an eye on her in the backseat, I wanted to pull that guy out of the car and give him a good thumping." Mom kept asking, "What did she do?" I knew I was going to be in big trouble when he answered that question, but he never answered her. He just said, "Never again." But, after we both got married we went on several double dates together with our spouses.

For any girl who's had **younger brothers**, you'll know what I mean, when I say, they are a Royal Pain. They follow you around like puppy dogs and nip at your heels. Chris is three years younger than me, and his favorite pastime was to get me into trouble. He'd lie if the need arose, and of course he felt the need arose quite often. One time he told mom I was behind the house kissing a boy. It was not true, but for the next few weeks, he was my constant companion, so that he might keep an eye on me. I had an uncle (different than the previously mentioned one) who was a police officer, and he gave my dad a can of mace (this was when mace was new on the market), I was messing around with it and sprayed Chris in the face. He started screaming bloody murder. I got scared, because I knew I was in deep trouble, so I sprayed myself (I know that was dumb), so now I'm screaming. Dad knowing what happened started laughing so hard, if I hadn't been in so much pain I would have been mad at him. He said, "All you can do is get air on your face and wait for the burn to wear off." So here goes two kids running around the outside of the house, screaming as if they were on fire, and they were. It did eventually wear off, and I didn't get in trouble, so the self-punishment worked.

My **baby brother** was a quiet, sweet boy. I remember when Mom brought him home from the hospital; our house sat on top of a steep hill, and I stood at the top as I watched Mom climb out of the cab carrying that little bundle. I was five when he  was born. He loved throwing everything over the hill—balls, toy cars, anything he got his hands on. We all guarded our possessions from Lee. When he was 3 or so, Chris came into the house and said, "Mom, Lee drove the car over the hill." She absently said, "He did", and continued husking corn. Chris said, "Mom, Lee drove **your** car over the hill." She and I dropped our corn at the same time and took off running. Fortunately, the car went to the left and came to rest at the foot of the hill against the embankment, if it had gone the other way, the car would have rolled over a steeper hill and probably would have killed him. **Boys** love play in and around cars, and other equipment—tractors, mowers, anything that moves. No matter how old Lee got he was still our baby brother. I bossed him around. I made both of the younger boys eat my mud pies. If they needed a third person to play, they'd have to obey me first. I was a mean older sister, but I loved them very much, and no one else would ever touch them if I could help it. One time I did get pretty sadistic. I was around 14, and Mom was doing a short run to the store. She left me in charge. The minute she pulled out of the drive; I got one of Dad's belts and told them to get on the couch and not to move. I said, "Mom's gone, and I'm in charge now, so you better sit there and not move a muscle." Of course, you know what happens when you tell boys not to move. Every time they moved, I swatted them. When Mom got home, they both told on me and then I was the one getting swatted. But it was worth it.

**

Husbands are **big boys**. I think the only reason they buy their sons remote control cars, race tracks, and train sets is so they can play with them.

I think it is true that the main difference between boys and men are the size of their toys. At one time my husband played with trucks in the dirt and now he drives and eighteen wheeler. He still loves to laugh and play. Just like a little boy, he likes to pick on me.

I'm so proud of all that he has done over the years, especially the way he raised out children.

Some husbands teach their sons to love and respect women, and the elderly. Mine taught our son to be respectful. They teach work ethics and the facts of life, the best they can.

My tween had picked up a pack of prophylactics. I discovered the little silver packet in his underwear drawer. I told my husband, "You are going to have to talk to him." He agreed. I listened at the bedroom door, this is what he said, "Son, don't hide something like this in your underwear drawer, you know your Mom's going to be in there, and she'll find them." Good talk.

My husband loved doing things with our son, like playing ball, attending all the games he could, bowling, and teaching him to drive.

This brings me to my **son**. Eternally funny, sharp-witted,  and deep. Left-handed, even walking left foot first when he started walking. He had to learn a lot on his own since I was not left-handed. He was great in art, music, and sports. Since each chapter starts with a little clip from **Tom's** first 12 years, I will continue on with year 13 through15. Popular and rotten, he always surrounded himself with a lot of friends and he kept an eye out for things he could get into that wouldn't get him in a lot of trouble if he got caught. He was hyperactive from the day he was born and constantly had to be on the go. He was a night owl and could function on very little sleep. I'm not sure when he turned from Tommy to Tom, but it gradually happened, and he liked girls who were unattainable.

When they built a new waterslide in our city, the kids wanted to go. I didn't have the money right then. It just so happened that Brenda pulled one of her back teeth during that time. Tom said, "If you will just pull three more teeth, with the money you get from them, we can both go on the waterslide." He was always quick witted, even if other people, such as his sister, didn't always appreciate his wit.

Alcohol and tobacco, he tried them both. Tom had gone home with some friends from church, and he sat up front with the other kids during the service. After the worship service, we waited at the door for him and his sister. He smiled at the adults and even shook hands with the preacher before exiting. I thought this was a bit strange, but hey, he was a teen—they change daily. When he entered the car, his dad and I looked at each other. His dad turned around and said, "Blow." **Tom's** breath about knocked us over. We were on our way to eat at a restaurant, so we continued on our journey. His dad tormented him, and I went along with it. We voiced our disapproval, but not in a real harsh way, since this was his first time consuming alcohol (that we knew of). He was not allowed to go home with kids from church for a while. We never had any other problems with alcohol.

I got the shock of my life when I moved my fourteen-year-old son's bed and 4 pouches of tobacco fell to the floor.

When he came home, I asked him, "Why did you buy all these pouches of tobacco?"

He said, "They were on sale."

I saw no humor in his answer. He got no extra money, nor was he allowed out of my sight for a long time. Boys, are going to push the limits.

A memorable year developed when Tom turned 16. He helped his dad and me in our ministry. As administrators for The Salvation Army, we wore many hats and so did Tom. He helped to teach the Sunday school classes, and the youth groups. He did pick-ups for our church activities, as well as pick-ups for the Thrift Store. He helped to keep the house clean, and the yard mowed. He developed a keen sense of honestly.

One time he went after a newspaper. He put in his money and came home with two newspapers. I explained to him about stealing is stealing, no matter how small the item, and to reinforce this I had him to take his own money, get back in his van, go back to the paper machine, open it up, and put the paper back. He protested the whole way. "Stupid, this is just stupid, lots of people do take more than one. I won't do it again. I don't have to go back to the machine." I just listened to him as we drove to the store. As parents, we need always to be on the lookout for opportunities to teach our children right from wrong.

Tom liked to procrastinate, and homework received the most procrastination from him. When he didn't finish his homework, he prayed about it. He came into the dining room just beaming. I asked, "Did you finish your homework?" He said, "No, but I prayed we wouldn't have school tomorrow." Of course, I insisted he do his homework, and of course he did not get it done since it was a project, and not a one night lesson he could do. The next day he got up and yelled into my room. "School's been canceled." I ran to the window and looked out there was no snow. I said, "You get to school." He laughed, and said, "School's canceled. Turn on the news." I did, and the newscaster informed me the water lines had burst at the school. School was canceled for two weeks, and then it went into Christmas break. His prayer turned into his being home for a month. He finished the project the day before school started back in.

We were transferred to a new town during **Tom's senior year**. He had a hard time picking subjects since his previous school had offered so much more in the subjects he was interested in. He ended up butting heads with a shop teacher, who imbibed in alcohol during class time. Again we found ourselves in the principal's office; this hadn't happened for a few years. Tom voiced how unfair the teacher behaved, and the teacher voiced how unresponsive Tom acted in his class. I tried to get him out of the class, but it was too late in the year. The teacher had said and done some things toward Tom, that were not professional. I told the principal, the one thing I knew about my son, was that he was very truthful. If he said something wrong happened, it happened. The principal of course defended the teacher, until I threatened to call in some of Tom's classmates. The teacher admitted his guilt and apologized. They tolerated each other the rest of the year.

Tom loved soccer and did great in it. He led his team through high school and earned some scholarship offers. An American Soccer team formed and the opportunity to travel abroad came about for Tom, but since we had to come up with a large amount of money, he refused to join the team. He graduated at 17 and decided to work a year, and then go to college. I tried to talk him into going straight to college, but he had his mind made up. He worked for a few years and then decided to get married, again I tried to convince him to go to college, but he said they would go together. A couple of years later he gave me an adorable little baby boy.

Life with a boy is a challenge, but the benefits of

having a wonderful loving, respectful, and caring son are more valuable than any amount of work that goes into raising a child. We are very proud of the man our son grew to be.

**

Grandchildren is my favorite word. I have received so much joy from them. I'll limit myself to a short, comical section per boy. I also have a granddaughter, but that is a different book.

The same year our son got married; our daughter gave us our first **grandson, Brad.** I never thought it would be possible to love a child as much as I loved my own children until I saw Brad being born. We lived in Florida during this time, but it didn't take long for us to make the decision to move back to West Virginia, and I have never regretted it. We have to make sacrifices to be near our children and grandchildren. It isn't possible for everyone, but we did a lot of praying and God made it possible for us.

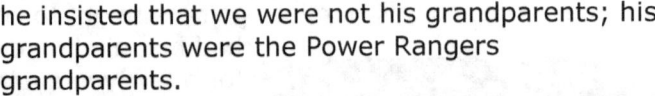

Around 2 years old **Brad** so loved the Power Rangers that he insisted that we were not his grandparents; his grandparents were the Power Rangers grandparents.

During this same time period, I asked Brad what he wanted to be when he grew up. He said, "A Nastic." That was a new one on me. I said, "What does a Nastic do?" He said, "You know; they jump on bars and do flips." I said, "Oh, Gymnastics." He said, "Yeah, that's what I say."

When he turned two, I sat him in his high chair and handed him a brush and paints. He painted some interesting pictures. When he started preschool, he had a hard time finger painting. He said, "Nah, I use a brush."

Then a little farther along; I was walking him through the store and he asked, "Mammaw, do fish bite?" I said, "No, fish

don't bite." He said, "Fish don't bite?" I said, "No, fish don't bite." He looked at me with a quizzical expression and said, "I ask Pappaw."

A quiet, calm boy, Brad learned quickly, by the time he turned 3 he had memorized all of the stories in a thick Children's Bible.

As the years passed, he loved to spend time with his Pappy, and learned to fish and carve wood.

Around 9, Brad wanted to please all of the adults in his life. He said he wanted to be a Preacher/truck driver/artist. Preacher for his grandpa, truck driver for his dad, and artist for me.

Brad, another child, much like his Uncle Tom, did and said funny things without trying to be funny. During one weekend, in his 12th year, he seemed to be getting bored, so I decided to search through my VCR tapes to see if I had something a young boy would enjoy. Finally I found a Shirley Temple movie the Bluebird; it had a little boy in it, so I thought he'd enjoy this show. He said, "Mammaw, that's old." I said, "It's not that old." He said, "It was probably made before 1992." His favorite movie was Halloween Town.

From an early age he enjoyed magic. And became pretty good at it. He enjoyed entertaining people. One time he stuck a large nail up his nose. He thought it was hilarious, but it was scary for the rest of us to watch, and a little sickening.

He tried different sports, but he favored skateboarding. He became good at doing tricks on the skateboard and traveled many miles on his boards over several years. **Brad** graduated, got a good job that he loves, got married and had a **baby boy**.

**

Andrew is my middle **grandson**. I'll always remember the pride on my **Son's** face as we watched the birth of his **son**. Sweet and amusing, Andrew busted into life, winning the hearts of everyone he met. When he was very small, I'd say, "Give Grandma your charming look." To my amazement, he'd give me this little crooked smile, and roll his eyes. He loved Ninja Turtles. He loved everything about them. We colored in many Ninja turtles coloring books for hours and hours.

Like his older cousin, and his dad anything with a ball caught his attention, but by the time he turned 5, he was great at soccer. He could run that ball down the field faster than anyone else in his age group.

Andrew loved to tell me about the happenings in his life. He said, "Lasterday, I rode in my car." I said, "You did?" He said, "Yeah, lasterday I had fun with my dad."

He didn't like leaving his mom and dad, but he loved to come to my house to visit, so he'd always want to go home with them. When his younger sister came along, in this tiny, precious voice he said, "Grandma, can we spend the night?" I'd said, "Of course." He giggle, and make a fist, raise his arm and pull it down, then yell, "Yes!" He'd run around the room playing with the toys, just as happy as could be. Then his parents would start putting their coats on to leave, and he'd run and get his coat. He said, "Rachel's staying here, and I'm going with you." At first, we tried to talk him into staying, but after a couple of times of either us taking him home, or his parents coming and getting him, we gave up.

He loved to dance and do little skits with me, but he was extremely bashful in front of anyone else. He just hated preforming at school.

We worked a lot of jigsaw puzzles together. It was so exciting when we found a hard to place piece.

He started playing video games before he could talk, and he still has a passion for them. He loves to watch sports on TV. His favorite team is from Florida.

Andrew, the most bashful of my grandsons, got a girlfriend at an earlier age than the other two did. His first serious relationship lasted a long time for a young boy. I thought it was so cute.

Even though Andrew, turns red easy, and hates being up front, he loves to giggle, and laugh. He banters with his grandpa, and loves to torment me. He likes to torment anyone, but especially the females in his life.

He played soccer almost all the way through school and has coached a team. He also loves to play basketball, but he never played it much in school. Now Andrew stays up most nights playing video games and mostly works the afternoon shift. He stays busy, but he always finds time to visit with his grandparents.

He often spends the night now. And he is still the sweetest young man, and he's still giggly and turns read easily.

**

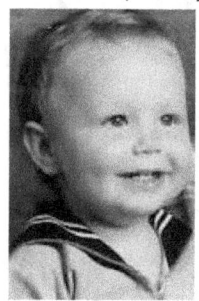

Ben, the youngest and wildest of the **boys**, kept us totally entertained. He made up songs and sang them from a very early age. He'd get so excited and went on full speed all the time, so of course he got injured often. He loved to climb trees and to be a daredevil, he'd climb all the way to the top. Fortunately when he fell out of the tree in my back yard, it was a Pine tree, and it wasn't as tall as some of the other trees. He started screaming, "I broke the wire in my neck. I broke the wire in my neck." I didn't laugh about this statement until later when I was sure there wasn't anything broken. Another time he got a big bump on his forehead. I said, "You're going to have a big goose egg tomorrow." The next day he came to visit, and he said, "Mammaw, you were so right. I got a big chicken knot." He pointed to his forehead. Again, I showed sympathy at the time, but to this day I think that's funny.

Ben had an imaginary friend, "Old Dead Grandpa". He and Old Dead Grandpa would go fishing, and on long walks. Ben would say, "Today, me and Old Dead Grandpa went down to the creek, and we found rocks."

At five, Ben started kindergarten, and he told me. "I'm done." I said, "What do you mean you're done?" He said, "I turned 5; I got homework, and I got a woman." He couldn't say girl very well.

One time, after we'd started driving a truck, we were away from home, and we talked to the grandkids on the phone as often as possible. During a conversation with Brad, we learned that **Ben** got put on the wall, a punishment his teacher gave him

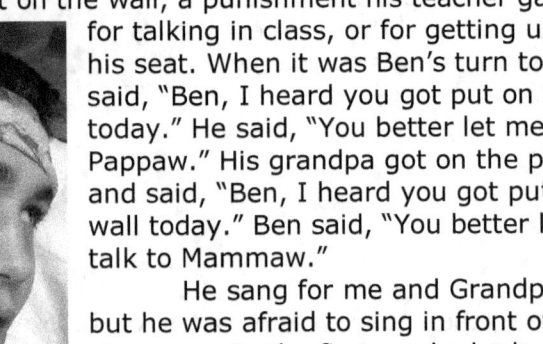

for talking in class, or for getting up from his seat. When it was Ben's turn to talk, I said, "Ben, I heard you got put on the wall today." He said, "You better let me talk to Pappaw." His grandpa got on the phone and said, "Ben, I heard you got put on the wall today." Ben said, "You better let me talk to Mammaw."

He sang for me and Grandpa a lot, but he was afraid to sing in front of strangers. In the first grade, he had a day that was very good, and his teacher said, "Ben, you've been really good today, what can I do for you to reward you?" Ben said, "I'll sing a song." And he did. That afternoon he told me about singing in class. I said, "I thought you were afraid to sing in front of people." He said, "Mammaw, sometimes you just have to face your fears." I've tried to remember that throughout the years.

Ben started playing soccer at age 5, and played all the way through school. He played very good. Singing remained a passion for him. He performed in front of the people in the small

church we went to a few times when he was 16 and 17. Major Payne has remained one of his favorite movies. Right now Ben is serving in the Army. I thank him for his service and look forward to giving him one of the biggest hugs he's ever received when he returns home.

I'm trying to talk him into going to American Idol when he gets out.

**

When I'd have all the **grandsons** together, and they'd start fussing at each other, especially in the car, I'd have them to help me make up little ditties. They'd get so caught up in making up the little songs they'd forget to argue with each other. One of the songs we made up went something like this. "Uncle Lee climbed a tree and skinned his knee. Oh meeee!" Then it'd be "I like to swing so high I can touch the sky. Oh myyyyy!" We'd go on and on making up verse after verse until we reached our destination.

We did a lot of walking, my grandsons and I. This was and still is my favorite times with them. Sometimes we're in a group, but usually it's a one on one experience. It's just a nice relaxing time. They get my full attention, and I get their full attention.

My best way to handle my grandkids was to bribe them. It worked with all four of them.

**

Along came **Mitch,** my **great-grandson**. I'll always remember the pride and joy in my oldest grandson's voice as he said, "Grandma, I'm going to be a dad." And then later he told me, "Grandma, I'm going to have a son." And then later he told me he'd picked out a strong, manly name for his boy, **Mitchell Curtis**.

I love how Brad kept me in the loop, and I love watching him play with his boy.

Mitch's great-grandpa and I held him right after he was born, and all the love you can possibly have for a baby came rushing from us to this little boy.

He's a happy, good baby. He doesn't fuss much, and it's easy to get him to laugh. He's already got a strong personality, and he's not even six months old. I love holding him, and reading to him. I can't wait until we can dance and sing together, and until we can go on walks together.

I am, and always have been surrounded by boys. I'm so blessed.

The following is a fictional story based on a true facts. It has been added to this Anthology, because it shows a father's devotion and the willingness of a stranger, who was raised well, to help a man in need. This also shows a man, who was raised well, but who got deranged somewhere along the line. Boys grow into men—sometimes good— sometimes bad.

Augusta's Main Memory
By Cher'ley Grogg

Air brakes squealed and pashinged as the driver pulled over to the side of the road. "End of the trail, partner." He shook his passenger awake. "My name's Jake, I didn't catch your name before you conked out."

The rider stretched his lean arms and uncoiled his long, skinny legs. He blinked slowly and looked at Jake as if he were from outer space. He rolled his eyes up toward the ceiling of the truck. "My name is Augusta. Augusta Maine."

"Sure buddy, maybe they named the next city after you." He laughed, reached across the stranger and popped open the passenger door. "Be seeing you Augusta, hope you find your daughter. What did you say her name was?"

Augusta mumbled something the truck driver couldn't understand, grabbed the big duffel bag that lay between the seats, and climbed down from the truck. He looked at the man before taking the last step onto the paved road. "Thanks Jake. I appreciate the ride."

"Say, Gus. You need a couple of bucks." Without waiting for an answer, Jake pulled a twenty from   his shirt pocket and handed it down to Augusta.

His ruddy complexion turned a little redder as he clasped onto the bill. He was still foggy from sleep, but he was sure he needed it. Why else would he be hitching a ride and where had he come from? "Thanks again. Ahh...Jake, where did you pick me up?"

Now Jake looked at him as if he were from outer space. "I picked you up in Hartford, Connecticut. You said, you thought you had to find your daughter; thought she was kidnapped; said the cops wouldn't look for her 'cause she'd done turned eighteen."

"Of course, sorry, I'm still a little groggy." Augusta rubbed his right eye with one finger. "Sure, did I happen to say why I thought she was kidnapped or by whom?"

"The only other thing was you showed me a faded snapshot and a beat up postcard. How long you been a-searchin' for her?"

"Not sure. Better be on my way." Augusta nodded and waved at the big rig before he turned and headed on down the highway. He heard the driver blow his air-horn, and he swiveled his head quick enough to catch sight of the dust, which followed the Kenworth down a side road.

He walked and thought. *Gosh must still be asleep. Can't remember anything. I have a daughter. Snapshot, photograph?* He started feeling his pockets and found a key chain with three keys, seventy-eight cents—no quarters, a pocketknife, and half a ticket stub. One key was a car key for a Chevrolet; the next one looked like a house key, and the third was for a lock—a padlock. *Can't remember? What's wrong with me?* He hoisted his army-green, four-foot long, duffel bag from his hands to his shoulder. It was stuffed full and heavy. *Need to look inside. Not here.* He walked further up Route 201 until he spotted a sign for Peacock Beach State Park. He'd stop there, use their facilities and then check inside his bag to see if there were some clues to his life.

He looked down at his feet. Even though, his black sneakers were well worn, they didn't have any holes in them. His jeans fit well and appeared clean. He wore a button up denim shirt. He ran his hand through his hair. It was a little long, but far from shoulder length. He pulled some down from the top, so he could see it. Light brown, sun bleached and dried. Conditioner surely would be a luxury. He smelled his armpit. Smelled fresh, like clean linen. At least he was able to shower and use deodorant. Caressing his chin divulged a day or two's worth of stubble. Maybe he had money stashed in his duffel. Maybe his car had broken down. He pushed his hair back and felt an indention in his skull. Not sore. Must be an old injury. From what?

He walked under the wooden arc that welcomed visitors into the park. A pavilion containing eight picnic tables sat on the left with two grills nearby. There were several single tables and grills farther out toward the woods. A semi-modern bathroom sat on the right, up a little grade and in front of a play area. A couple of little kids were swinging, and their mother watched from a nearby park bench.

This park had a familiar feel to it, but all state parks are similar. He cocked his head to hear a Black-capped Chickadee. A Parus Atricapillus, omnivorous. Maine's state bird. It wasn't actually singing, because its 'tshe, daigh daigh daigh' would not be considered a song. It was an angry rasping. Augusta didn't have a picnic lunch, which was good because he didn't want to share it with the little Chickadee. This timid bird became aggressive when it came to food. Eat like a bird took on a different meaning with these birds. Am I a bird watcher? No— doesn't feel right. However, I know that the Black-capped Chickadee is also the state bird of Massachusetts. How?

He didn't have time to worry about birds. He had a missing daughter. Name unknown, age unknown, appearance unknown, but he knew she was real and she was in trouble.

Exhaling deeply from frustration caused him to inhale just as deeply which filled his nostrils with a fresh, earthy smell and he could hear water running, maybe a waterfall or a river rushing on its way downstream. A small sign pointed to a trail, and it read Cobbosseecontee Stream. *Hmm, whitewater rafting.* Did he raft? He'd check the stream out after his bathroom break. It'd offer him some privacy; he didn't want to open his bag in front of anyone.

His mind continued working as he ran water over his hands. Maine state motto Dingo means—I lead. Pine tree state, 23rd state, capital Augusta. Augusta Maine. That can't be my name. Truck driver probably thought I was crazy. Am I?

Hollow light colored eyes looked back at him. The piece of tin that served as a mirror distorted his image. Blue, maybe grey or hazel didn't matter—were his daughter's eyes light colored too?

The June sun caused him to blink rapidly when he exited the building. He headed toward the Cobbosseecontee Stream sign. Hopefully there would be a picnic table under the canopy of the woods. His heart rate quickened, and his breathing became rapid. Not from the walk--his long stride was effortless, but from anticipation. He heard a woman screeching. Was this his daughter's voice? Real—close by. He heard it again. It wasn't in his head. It was real. He juggled his duffel and cannonballed down the trail.

"Help, help! My son's drowning." A small woman had her arms wrapped around a young boy—five or six years old—who was caught fast in the branches of a fallen tree. The rushing water pulled on his legs and she pulled on his chest. His head lolled to the side, and his complexion was a pale greenish-blue. The water splashed into his face. The mother had slid under the boy, and the roaring stream beat against her face, but she never stopped yelling and she never let go. She'd yell for help and then she'd whisper in the boy's ear. "Hold on Jimmy. Mommy's here Jimmy."

He's dead. She'll be next. He dropped his bag and pulled off his shoes. He felt he should try to save the mother first and then worry about the boy.

Instantly the wild water knocked him off his feet. The rocks were mossy and slick. He caught himself, eased further downstream, grabbing whatever was close by to stay upright. "Hold on. I'm here," he yelled. Could she hear him over the deafening noise? "I'm coming."

In what seemed like hours, but in actuality was a few minutes, he reached the mother and son. He pulled on her, but she held her son tightly with her right arm, as she struck at him with her left. She vigorously shook her head. "Get Jimmy." She clasped her son again. Again, he tugged at her, and she tried to head-butt him. "Get Jimmy."

Augusta had no choice. He released the mother and grabbed the boy. Even though, the water had a tight grip, the boy was buoyant and light. The mother continued to hang onto him while Augusta untangled his legs and arms from the branches. The woman slipped and went under. He grabbed her one-handed and draped her over the fallen tree. She was weak but conscious. "Can you hang onto my waist?" He didn't know if her legs were damaged, but she didn't seem to be able to support herself. He knew if he left her long enough to get the child to the bank, she'd be gone.

She nodded and circled her arms around his waist. As

carefully as possible, he carried the boy and drug the woman
from the water. He laid the son on the bank, reached behind
himself, and pulled the woman up. Immediately he started CPR.

He sensed there was danger in giving mouth-to-mouth, but
there was no choice. He opened the boy's mouth and checked for
any foreign bodies in the airway; finding none, he began chest
compressions. 1, 2, 3...30, rest—recheck airway. 1,2,3...30,
stop—readjust head. 1, 2, 3...14, 15. The boy sputtered and
coughed.

The mother crawled up to them and laid her head on his
chest. She held his tiny off-colored hand.

Help was still needed and fast. He rolled the boy on his side,
so that if he spit up any more water he wouldn't swallow it
again. "I need to get help. I'll be back."

"Hurry, please hurry." She reached out for him.

"I will." He ran up the trail and stopped a young couple.

"Got a cellular phone?"

They looked at the wet, out of breath, bare-footed man and
drew back.

He put his hands on his knees and raised his head because
his breath came in spurts. "There's a boy, he's dying. Need
911."

The young man unsnapped his cell from his belt and handed
it to Augusta. Augusta waived it away. "Call 911."

He stumbled back to the mother and son. The couple stood
in shock for a few seconds and then followed.

"Give me your shirt." Augusta pointed to the man's shirt. Still
extremely out of breath he gasped, "Take boy's clothes off. Rub
arms and legs." He looked at the young woman. "Rub mother.
Warm her up."

The young woman paused, "Are you a doctor?"

"I'm Au...I'm Gus."

"Gus, thank you. You saved his life." The mother mumbled
and cradled the child.

A siren blasted over the sound of the rushing water. Gus
eased away. He grabbed his duffel and his shoes and headed off
in a direction away from the path. Am I a doctor or a medic? I
knew just what to do. He looked at his hands, no calluses. He
didn't want to face any people of authority until he found out who

he was, what he was doing hitching rides along strange highways and why he was searching for his daughter.

He still needed to find a secluded picnic table and he hoped he had clean, dry clothes in his bag.

The rickety table tottered as he sat down. He bounced as he sat to see if it would support his weight, then he swung one leg over the bench. He unzipped his duffel and started pulling out clothes and papers, a big manila envelope filled a side pocket and something else--he pushed on the bag--something hard. Goodnight! A gun. He forced the gun as deep as he could, grabbed a T-shirt and stuffed it on top of the gun. He supposed there was ammo in there too, but he'd check that out later.

He peeled off his clothes, emptied his pockets, redressed in a clean pair of jeans and a button-up dress shirt. He got some dry socks and pulled his sneakers onto his feet. The wet clothes were hung in a nearby tree.

He felt certain, the mother and son would be okay, but what about his daughter, Amelia.

Amelia, that was her name. Or at least he thought it to be her name or was he thinking of Amelia Earhart. He seemed to have a lot of facts floating through his mind. He could remember all kinds of things, just not the things that were the most important in his life. He tried to think of a wife. The young helper had a wife.

Gus thought of Amelia Earhart and remembered why he'd named his daughter Amelia. She proved that men and women were equal in "jobs requiring intelligence, coordination, speed, coolness and willpower." He hoped someday his daughter would set records and get recognition like the one Earhart received after her flight on May 20, 1932 from Harbor Grace, Newfoundland to Paris. Somehow, he felt his Amelia shared the courage and skill of her namesake. He needed to find her.

He flattened the ticket stub and placed the keys beside it. He glanced through the loose papers. The first thing he picked up was a newspaper from Rhode Island, Augusta shuddered at the headlines 'Two teenage girls face child pornography charges after posting sexually explicit photographs of themselves on the Internet.' He prayed no one would post explicit photos of Amelia. He prayed hard for his daughter and for the two girls in the headlines. He prayed his memory would return. Maybe there would be a Bible among his possessions with a name in it. He could be a minister, they knew about current events and history. This idea gave him a small amount of comfort.

The next paper item was a restaurant receipt from Burger King in Portsmouth, New Hampshire. There, he just gobbled some food and went on.

The final thing in this bunch of papers was a business card from a Laundromat in Massachusetts. He thought for a couple of seconds, and an image came to his mind. A woman had talked to him; told him about criminals who were cutting off their monitoring bracelets. A lovely woman, with a different name like his, Hank.

Hank said, "This man was convicted of child pornography. This man of assault and battery. He's charged with possession of drugs. This one with dealing drugs, impersonating a police officer. Assault and battery." She had photos. No, no-not talking to me. She was on TV-a reporter.

He needed to find the photo of his daughter; the trucker said he had showed him a photo.

Augusta hurriedly popped open the big envelope and shook out the contents. Out fell a scarred photo and a dilapidated postcard. He looked hard at the photo. The young girl smiled showing both rows of teeth. She had light brown hair and blue eyes. 16, 17 maybe—school photo. Probably not recent. Amelia. He turned it over, and there was some writing on the back. 'Daddy, I love you.' I love you too, Pumpkin.

The postcard simply read. "You're daughter's good. She's doing what she wants. Leave her be." The postmark was smudged, but Augusta could make out the ME that stood for Maine.

He stared at the picture. There had to be a way for him to remember this girl. Whoever wrote that postcard had her, and Augusta didn't believe she wanted to be there.

Keys to a car, a house and a padlock, half a ticket, a photograph and a postcard totaled his world. And the gun. He hadn't forgotten the gun. Did he know how to use it? He looked around. No one in sight. He unzipped the side pocket and touched the Glock 19. Without pulling it the rest of the way out he knew, it was his gun, and he was very familiar with it. Owning a gun, a Glock, does not make me a cop. It doesn't make me a crook either.

Then he got worried. His daughter may be missing because he was a crook. She may have been taken to prove something to him. To force him into doing something.

A crackle, full alert status, something coming down the trail.

"Gus, how you doing? That's was great, what you did with little Jimmy. He's okay. His mom is doing good too. "

Augusta recognized the young man who had assisted him and woman who clung to his arm, but all he heard was "is doing good". The postcard said, 'Your daughter is doing good'.

"Gus, you okay?"

His eyes widened in wonderment. An epiphany—how long he'd searched for his memory he didn't know, like a key that fits an unusual lock, the words that Tad spoke opened Augusta's main memories, and they came so rapidly he could barely process them. Those words, those familiar words—'Your daughter is doing good'—the postcard was from someone he knew and the feeling he had about Amelia being in danger, just heightened.

A quick explanation to Tad and then I'd be on my way to save my precious daughter. "I'm not Gus. I'm not Augusta Maine. I'm Matthew Thomas, and I teach History and American Studies. I have a lovely wife, Charlene and a brilliant daughter Amelia. I'm sorry, I'd love to stay and visit, but I must be on my way. My daughter is in danger." Matthew started stuffing his belongings back in the duffel. "Oh dear."

"What's wrong professor?"

"I don't have a car. I had a 67 Camaro; someone crushed my skull in and took the car."

"We'll take you to the hospital."

"I'm fine now. I had a temporary lapse of memory, but I'm fine now. My daughter is missing. I must rescue her."

"You know where she is? We'll take you." He turned to his wife. "Won't we Sharon?" She nodded.

"Really, I'll make it worth your effort." He grabbed his clothes from the trees and stuffed them in on top of the rest of his

clothes. Didn't matter now if they were wet or not. "Let's hurry."
He rushed ahead of the couple. The trail seemed much rougher
and steeper going back up, than it had on his way down. The dirt
and fine gravel spewed from under his sneakers, but that didn't
slow him down.

Matthew stopped at the top and waited on the young couple.

"We're parked over there, the silver escort. Not much to look
at, but she'll get us to where we're going." The young man
practically drug his wife to the car. He said something to Sharon
and she got in the backseat. He opened
the trunk.

Matthew tossed his duffel in the
trunk, but held the lid open. "What's
your name?"

"Nice to meet you sir." Tad held out
his hand.

"Thank you, Tad." He nodded at the
trunk. "Could you give me a minute?"

"I'll be in the car."

Matthew immediately got the gun,
checked the magazine and put it in the
front pocket of his pants. The gun
touched the key chain, and he realized
the padlock key went to his gun cabinet. Wasting no time, he
rushed around the car and climbed in--one long leg at a
time. The car was a tight squeeze for him, but that didn't matter;
he was thankful he had a ride.

"Where to Professor?"

"Do you know how to get on Interstate 95?"

"Sure."

"Head north."

Matthew hoped to reach his daughter before anything
happened to her. He prayed that his hunch was right. The police
wouldn't look for her because she was just 2 weeks away from
her 18th birthday, and she had already graduated from high
school. In fact, she had a good start on college. She'd been
taking college courses since her junior year. She was happy. She
wouldn't have left without talking to her parents. Glad Charlene
didn't come. Need to call her.

"Tad, may I use your cellular phone?"

The young man unclipped his phone and handed it to Matthew. Matthew dialed his home number, and Charlene answered on the first ring.

"I'm fine. Have you heard from Amelia?" Matthew's face didn't show a lot of emotion, but his jaw twitched as he listened to his wife tell him that she had not heard from their daughter. She felt as if she was having a nervous breakdown. Where had he been? Did he know anything about her baby?

"I will explain the whole matter to you when I...when we get home. Goodbye, now, Charlene." Matthew had tears in his eyes and a hard knot in his throat. His wife said she had her sister there and that she loved him. "I feel the same way. Goodbye now." I love you, Charlene. I even love your name. But, right now, I have to think of our little girl. He handed the phone back to Tad.

His atlas was in his Camaro, but he'd memorized the location. He was sure his neighbor's doped-up son, Harold, was behind this whole thing. The well-respected parents had raised him the right way, but he got mixed up in a bad crowd, left home, and he went off the deep end. He always said he'd be back for Amelia; he said when she turned 18; he'd be back for her. Matthew thought of him as a boy, but he was 29. Eleven years older than her--Amelia was only 10 when he first came home from a camping trip and declared his love for her. Charlene would never allow him around Amelia alone. He'd slipped over a couple of times, and Charlene had called the police. They said nothing could be done until Harold did something. That's when Matthew bought the Glock.

Matthew stared out the window. I should have killed him the first time he looked at Amelia. His face hardened, his eyes pinched down, and his mouth became a straight line above his chin.

"Professor, when was the last time you ate?"

"I'll eat when Amelia is safe. I've gone through too much to take any chances on missing them now. I had a temporary memory loss from the head- bashing; yet, I knew I had to keep moving north. I couldn't remember the exact address or my daughter's name. I didn't even know my name, but I knew danger lurked close by. Now that I know, the urgency is even greater. I don't know how long he'll keep her in Maine before he finds a way to cross into Canada. If he does that..."

"How long has it been since you talked to the police. Maybe the police in Maine are different from the police in Connecticut."

"I doubt it." He only trusted himself to get her back. Matthew stared straight ahead. "It's about 3 hours north, exit 264 to Highway 158. There are some rental cabins back in there, and a ways behind them is another cabin. He told his father that he owns it, but I doubt he owns anything. He gets his mail at a post office address. I made his dad give me specific directions. There should be plenty of daylight left when we get there. Then, if you wish to call the police, you may."

The rest of the trip was quiet. Tad tried to make small talk a

few times, but Matthew half-answered him and the conversation would die.

The hair raised on the back of his neck and everywhere else for that matter when Tad put on his signal light. They passed the

main set of cabins and the paved road stopped. Tad did too.

"I understand if you want me to walk from here." Matthew grabbed the door handle.

"Do you think this is a road?"

"It's dirt and not used often, but it's definitely a road."

"Onward we go."

When a slab of the cabin showed through the woods Matthew told Tad to stop the car.

"Wait here."

"I'd better come with you."

"It will be best for you to wait here. If I don't come back in 20 minutes, call the police. Do not come after me."

Matthew's stealthy footsteps seemed quieter than his heartbeat as he closed in on the cabin. Several chunks of wood were missing, and newspapers filled in the holes. The window had cardboard where glass had once been. The small porch had rotting boards and termite infested posts. Matthew searched for a way to peek inside. He could feel his daughter's presence. That meant that she was alive but in what condition?

He walked around the cabin until he spotted a hole where there was no newspaper. He peered inside. He saw Harold. The man's back was turned, and he knelt before the fireplace, but Matthew recognized him. A rustle came from the side of the room that Matthew couldn't see. His palms had water pouring from every pore. He reached in his pocket. It would only take a second to cock the gun. His right hand shook slightly. The Glock 19 was light enough to be aimed one handed or two. Matthew would use two. He'd never killed a living thing. His target practice was right on the money. Amelia's safety and rescue was all that mattered. He needed a better look. Needed to see her. He moved around the building. A window, with glass. He peeked inside.

Amelia spotted her father. He put his finger to his lips. She sat in a straight chair, the kind with arms, like an old office chair. Her legs were gracefully crossed; one hand lay in her lap, but the other was cuffed to the arm of the chair.

Matthew had to think quickly which was hard because, his mind still wasn't clear. There was much he couldn't remember, but he knew he faced life straight on.

He snuck up on the front porch, kicked the door open and yelled, "Freeze. Don't turn around."

Harold, half-rose.

"Get on your knees. Don't turn around. Hands in the air. Where's the key?"

Harold followed directions, but he didn't answer.

"Amelia, where's the key?"

"Oh, Daddy. It's in his pants pocket."

"Daddy?" Harold asked. He dropped his hands and rose to his feet at the same time. Just as he started to spin around a blast went off. He finished his rotation. He smirked and said, "Professor, you shot me. I didn't think you had it ..." That's as far as he got. He dropped to the floor.

Amelia screamed, "You've killed him."

Matthew didn't know if that was a bad thing or a good thing. All he knew was that he needed to get his daughter out of there. He knelt down on one knee to search Harold for the key. "He's still alive. He's just wounded in his shoulder."

As he was rising, with the key, he heard. "Freeze, hands in the air."

Finally, the police had come to do something about the situation, but they had the wrong man.

"No, don't shoot. That's my dad." Harold's the one who kidnapped me. He's the one... on the floor.

We're all going downtown.

Matthew held up the key. The officer motioned for him to go ahead. He set his daughter free and then gave her one of the longest hugs he had ever given anyone in his whole life. She was almost as tall as he was, but she was still his little girl. He remembered hugs from earlier years, he remembered the tears in her eyes as she got back on her bike, and the brave look on her face when she had to have stitches after falling off her skateboard. Many times, he had picked her up and hugged her, but never had he felt the relief that he felt at that moment.

"Daddy, I knew you'd come. I kept telling Harold you'd find me. He said there was no stinking way no one would come

a-lookin' this far out and he said you told him it was okay for me to be here with him."

"Pumpkin, you know that was a lie."

"I know. I knew you'd find me."

When Matthew didn't return on time, Tad followed the professor's instructions; waited where he was and called the police.

As they were leaving the cabin, the second cruiser stopped to let Matthew talk to Tad.

"We've got to go with this officer."

"We'll follow you down there, and then we'll take you home," Tad said.

Matthew swallowed hard; it had been an emotional day. He was overwhelmed with all that had happened, but he still recognized the kindness of this young couple; and the truck driver and perhaps others that he couldn't remember at the moment. He cleared his throat and said, "Tad may I use your cellular phone again. It would be proper for Amelia to call her mother."

When Amelia hung up, Matthew gave the phone back to Tad, climbed in the cruiser beside his daughter and rode to the police station.

Matthew told his story. It didn't take long for the police to clear Matthew and Amelia.

The police officer said, "Harold will be locked up here for now. He's looking at prison time."

"What about my Camaro?"

"It's probably in more states than you've traveled through these last few days."

As soon as they left the station and climbed into Tad's car. Matthew shifted his weight and said, "Amelia. I have something for you." He pulled the ticket stub from his pocket. "You won a bike helmet." Rubbing his head, he laughed and said, "I was the one that needed it."

Amelia giggled and laid her head on father's shoulder.

The Dog and His Reflection
An Aesop's Fable

A Dog, to whom the butcher had thrown a bone, was hurrying home with his prize as fast as he could go.

As he crossed a narrow footbridge, he happened to look down and saw himself reflected in the quiet water as if in a mirror. But the greedy Dog thought he saw a real Dog carrying a bone much bigger than his own.

If he had stopped to think, he would have known better. But instead of thinking, he dropped his bone and sprang at the Dog in the river, only to find himself swimming for dear life to reach the shore.

At last he managed to scramble out, and as he stood sadly thinking about the good bone he had lost, he realized what a stupid Dog he had been.

The moral of Aesops Fable: It is very foolish to be greedy.

Thoughts from Parents

Puberty starts anywhere from 9-14 and many changes take place.

Let your son know that some people will think that he sounds like his mom when he answers the phone. His voice will go up, down, high, and low before it settles into the voice he will have as and an older boy.

A boy will look at his armpits every day to see if he has at least one hair. It will be a day worthy of celebration when he discovers that hair.

Super-sensitive area, down yonder has a lot of nerve endings — which make it extra-sensitive — so if a soccer ball accidentally whams into a boy in that spot; it really hurts. The good news is that these injuries are not usually serious, though a boy will usually feel pain and even could be nauseated for a while. But always use caution.

Schools and doctors try to teach boys the correct words for their private parts, but it's doubtful that they will use those words, so be ready for the slang words.

If there isn't a man in the house, let your son know that Mom's know about men parts, or supply someone for him to talk to like a grandfather, uncle, or doctor. Boys have a lot of questions during the big changes their bodies go through. You could also go to the library together and look up his questions and then discuss them.

Get all the advice and instruction you can, so you will be wise the rest of your life. Proverbs 19:20 NLT

Chapter Eleven

Eleven was an age that was filled with self-expression for Tommy. He loved Tennis and was good at it. We saved up enough money to get him a very nice tennis racket for Christmas. The very first game we attended he got mad at himself for missing the ball and slammed his tennis racket onto the tennis court. I thought his dad was going to fall off the bleachers. We had a very long discussion that evening about taking care of your property.

Frank Larnerd

Frank was born in Knoxville, Tennessee and spent much of his childhood engrossed in weird stories of monsters, mutants, and other worlds. He has worked as a morgue night watchman, shoe salesman, and color commentator for IWA: East Coast wrestling.

Although he is best known for his unique blend of traditional Appalachian folklore and unsettling horror, Frank has also published numerous science fiction and crime stories.

Currently, Frank studies Professional Writing at West Virginia State University, where he has received multiple awards for fiction and non-fiction. He lives in Putnam County, West Virginia.

Contact information:

the_ghoul@live.com www.franklarnerd.com

Monster Spray
By Frank Larnerd

My little brother Dan couldn't fall asleep because of the Hand.

I was nine, and he was seven. We were living in Monsey, New York; about an hour's drive from the city. My mother and father paid a small fortune, even by today's standards for a two bedroom apartment with ugly paper thin walls. We lived on the third floor, without air-conditioning or an elevator.

One day, a family friend from church stopped by and somehow the subject of the conversation turned to ghosts.

Dan and I sat at the kitchen table and listened to the story of the Hand.

We were told that many years ago, Dutch settlers had a small community not far from where we were. One night, Indians, attacked the settlers. One of the men was caught out in the open. He ran for his cabin as the warriors chased after him. He was able to slip inside, but his wife had closed his hand in the door. An Indian brave cut off the hand with his tomahawk, and with his trophy, the Indians returned to their camp.

They had a great celebration; feasting and dancing late into the night. The Indian brave proudly displayed the hand and boasted of its capture. Before he slept, the brave tied the hand to the top of his lodge pole for everyone to see.

While the Indians celebrated, there was sorrow back at the Dutch settlement. Succumbing to loss of blood, the Dutchman died clutching his bloody stump.

After the Indian campfires had gone out, the fingers of the Hand began to move.

It untied itself first and then slid down the lodge pole like a spider. It crept in the shadows and scurried silently over the bed skins. The Hand crawled to the face of the sleeping Indian brave. It strangled him without a sound.

Under the moonlight, the Hand scrambled from teepee to teepee until it had strangled every man, woman and child in the Indian camp.

We were told that many years later, the spot was cleared for housing. At night, there were disturbances. Dozers had hoses yanked out. Backhoes were marked with fist shaped dents. A security guard was hired to keep watch. He was found in the morning, strangled in his sleep. Around the site, there were tracks that looked like hand prints.

The construction continued and over time an entire apartment complex was built on the site of the Indian camp. Now, we were living there.

The story freaked me out, but not like Dan.

While the Hand was out there, he couldn't fall asleep.

Every shadow was the Hand slinking closer and closer. Every sound was an impatient fingernail tapping, restlessly awaiting the chance to pounce.

While I slept on the other end of the room, Dan waited for the Hand to get him.

My mother soon found out about the Hand and my brother's groggy performance at school.

My mother tried tranquil bed time stories. She tried a nightlight with a plastic cartoon character. I think she even tried warm milk.

Still, Dan couldn't sleep.

One night, Dan, complained again about the Hand. Mom was out of ideas. So, my mother employed the great skill of mothers everywhere...

She lied with a straight face.

She told Dan that she had been given a recipe for monster spray. This mystic concoction was guaranteed to keep all monsters away, including the Hand. After tucking Dan back into bed, my mom filled a spray bottle with water and some of her formidable lavender perfume.

Mom squirted the monster spray around the room, paying extra attention to the closet and other spots where The Hand had been sighted. She told Dan that as long as he could smell the monster spray, it was working.

Dan slept that night and every night after that, but it was my mother's cleverness and lavender scent that assured us pleasant dreams.

Soldiers of Summer
By Frank Lanerd

It was war.

The locals boarded themselves in their homes, their prayers punctuated by explosions and gunfire. Overhead, bombers roared toward the south, heavy laden with ordinance. Intense shelling left smoking craters across the battlefield, scarring the ground and blackening the trees. Abandoned vehicles dotted the landscape, billowing out black flumes like signal fires of the apocalypse.

The soldiers lounged around a hastily constructed shelter, loading their weapons for the battle to come. Each one was festooned with dangerous armaments and bandoleros of neon ammunition. Their faces told of the ravages of war, spelled out in battle scars and vacant eyes. They stood on the edge of the jungle, nearly invisible in the thick foliage. Below them was a bullet-pocked apartment complex, still and silent before the coming conflict.

"Get set up, guys." Bentley said, shouldering his yellow Warfang 070. "They'll be here soon."

Randy pushed up his glasses and pointed toward the bivouac. "This place is probably full of poison ivy."

"Don't eat it then," Marshawn said as he brushed by him. He got down on his belly and shimmed through the shelter's narrow opening. "Hey, it's pretty cool in here."

Randy kneelt down and poked his head inside the narrow enclosure. "How does this work again?"

"God. We just went over this." Marshawn said, rolling his eyes.

Reaching out, Bentley grabbed the back of Randy's shirt and pulled him up. "It's assault, remember? If they take the base, they win, and we're dead."

Something moved near the corner of the apartments, and the soldiers ducked behind the bivouac, weapons at the ready. A stocky commando approached, dressed in tight fitting camouflage pants and a matching headband.

"Jesus," Randy said, breathing a sigh of relief. "It's just Pooter,"

Pooter shuffled closer, grinning like he'd eaten a hundred pixy sticks. "Hey, guys. Did you start yet?"

"What the heck is that?" Randy asked, pointing at Pooter's weapon.

The commando held a 3-foot-long battle rifle, its bright blue stock shimmering with newness. It had gyroscopic sights, an extended magazine, and attached to its mounting base was an enormous neon orange scope that could have doubled as a telescope.

"Boys, say hello to the X12 Stormhammer," Pooter said, pride beaming from his face.

Bentley said. "That's sick."

"Yeah," Pooter said. "My Eaglestrike got busted when Stevie knocked me down by the mail box."

Randy grabbed the rifle out of Pooter's hands and peered down its scope. "Forget the Eaglestrike. This thing is totally rocking." He pointed it toward the sun and made a series of "pew pew" noises.

Marshawn stuck his head out of the bivouac. "Come on! They're going be here any minute!"

"I'm ready," Randy said, sliding a magazine into his T21 Obliterator.

Pointing to the jungle's rising hillside, Bentley said, "Pooter, you keep us covered from up there." He nodded to the left. "Randy you take that side, I'll get the other."

Randy saluted. "Rodger that."

"What about me?" Marshawn asked.

Bentley cocked his rifle. "Keep them out, no matter what."

He scurried off, keeping behind the tree line as he moved into position. The shade was stronger here, nearly obscuring the blazing June sun. The scents of pine and earth rich and pungent among the cicadas summer song.

Bentley dove behind a poplar tree and flicked up the sights of his Warfang. To his right, Pooter puffed and wheezed up the hillside, dragging his Stormhammer behind him. Bentley shook his head and turned his attention to the apartment building.

It wasn't long before two troopers appeared, sweeping the area with their weapons as they crept forward. Bentley knew them, Dennis and his brother Jordan from 314 B. They wore matching Myrtle Beach tank tops jammed into pleated church pants. The big one wielded a green and purple J47 Nightclaw, while his younger brother cradled am Ironshot crossbow.

"That's right," Bentley whispered. "Just a little closer." He wrapped his finger around the Warfang's orange trigger, ignoring the beads of sweat that rolled down his face.

"They're coming!" Pooter voice echoed from the hillside.

Bentley cursed under his breath as the brothers threw themselves down and aimed in the direction of the alarm. On the other side of the bivouac, shots rang out as a second force moved in from the opposite side.

Randy leapt from his spot and open fired with his T21 Obliterator. "Come get some, you savages!"

He grit his teeth as he strafed the enemy's position. Streaks of orange shot from his gun, slicing through the underbrush in all directions. Again and again he fired, pelting the area with a barrage of neon fire. As his weapon kicked empty, Stevie stepped out from behind a sagging maple.

Stevie was the oldest soldier on the battlefield, his face already ravaged by angry red pimples. His shovel-toothed grin made him look half shark and half rodent as he peered down the sights of his modified 99 Hexblade. Sadistically calm, he squeezed the trigger.

"Ouch!" Randy yelled as the bolt slammed into his chest. He crumpled down onto the leaves, rubbing the spot where he was hit.

"I got you. I got you." Stevie snorted as he cocked another round into his rifle.

Randy looked up with one open eye. "I'm laying here dead, ain't I?"

"You ain't dead enough," said Stevie. He fired another shot that ricocheted off Randy's groin. "That's better."

Dennis and Jordan sprung from their cover and dashed toward the tree line. As they swung around an outcropping of pines, the pair became entangled in a patch of Scrub Oak. The twigs pulled at their clothes and snarled around their feet.

Bentley waited until they were halfway clear and fired. His shot hit Jordan in the guts, causing the younger brother to flop backward on his brother. As Dennis pushed his brother's body away, Bentley chambered another round.

Screaming, Dennis fired blind as he struggled to free his legs from the brush. His neon darts plunked harmlessly off the tree Bentley used for cover.

"Missed me!" Bentley shouted as he lunged out from the opposite side and fired.

Dennis flinched as the bolt struck his Adam's apple. Gurgling, he pressed his hands to the spot and slunk down beside his brother. Bentley raced past them, readying another shot as he ran.

Stevie stood at the mouth of the shelter, laughing as he pumping rounds into the opening. Inside, Marshawn cowered and screeched while the stinging bolts peppered his body.

"Knock it off!" Marshawn bawled.

Stevie laughed. "Does it hurt?"

Bentley burst from the jungle and leapt on top of the shelter. He aimed his Warfang down at Stevie. "I've been waiting for this!"

Steve raising his hands. "Alright, you got me. I surrender."

"Sorry, Stevie." Bentley growled. "I don't take prisoners,"

He fired. The bolt whipped forward, smacking Stevie between the eyes. The older soldier dropped to his side and lay motionless.

Bentley jumped down from the bivouac and shouted, "Pooter! Come down. I got them. We won!"

Leaves crackled as Pooters chubby body rolled down the hill. He came to a stop at Bentley's feet, eyes open, tongue hanging from the corner of his mouth. Bentley rushed to his side and gently cradled his head. A foam sword jutted out from his body, jammed between his arm and his ribs.

"Pooter, who did this?" Bentley asked.

The commando looked up at him with fading eyes. "Sorry, Bentley... Stormhammer jammed on me... There's one more..."

His words were cut off with a series of coughs. He trembled for a moment and lay quiet.

Bentley raised his clenched fists and screamed at the heavens. "Pooter!"

A pink dart fired from the shadows, striking Bentley in the temple. He moaned as he crashed backward to the jungle floor. After an appropriate death twitch, he looked up through squinted eyes. Standing over him was a fierce-eyed assassin wearing a black balaclava.

Bentley raised an eyebrow. "Olivia?"

The assassin pulled away her mask and shook her long ponytail free. "I got you, Bentley." Smiling, she helped him to his feet.

Bentley pointed at her weapon. "Cool gun. Is that a Witchraven 400?"

"500," Olivia said. "Got it for my birthday last week, along with Crime Spree 2 for the Playstation."

Bentley's mouth hung open. "You've got Crime Spree 2?"

"You can come over and play it if you want," Olivia said with a smile.

"Hey, Bentley!" Marshawn called.

The other soldiers had gathered around the bivouac, checking their weapons and dusting their clothes free of leaves. Bentley noticed Pooter fishing around in one of his nostrils.

"You ready to pick new teams?" Marshawn asked.

He turned back to the assassin. She smiled at him, the summer sun twinkling in her eyes.

"No," Bentley said, tossing his Warfang to the dirt. "I'm think I'm going to hang out with Olivia for a while."

Braves
By Frank Lanerd

War whoops and broken appliances
Legos left as midnight landmines
Toxic socks and unmade beds
Pronounced symptoms of chronic mania
Forgotten bubblegum and dirty nails
Squealing cartoon shows at dawn
Doritos and ice cream for dinner
Noble toothless jack-o'-lantern smiles
Inhuman gas and savage grunts
Weapons made from broken branches
Loud and fearless
Each one a member of my tribe

My Bike
By Frank Lanerd

My first bike was a girl's bike
That my stepfather spray-painted blue
My second bike was a chrome
I circled our trailer park without using my hands
My third bike was stolen
Brought back in pieces by hard-faced officers
My fourth bike is yours
So that you can learn to ride

The Man and the Serpent
An Aesops Fable

A Countryman's son by accident trod upon a Serpent's tail, which turned and bit him so that he died. The father in a rage got his axe, and pursuing the Serpent, cut off part of its tail. So the Serpent in revenge began stinging several of the Farmer's cattle and caused him severe loss. Well, the Farmer thought it best to make it up with the Serpent, and brought food and honey to the mouth of its lair, and said to it: "Let's forget and forgive; perhaps you were right to punish my son, and take vengeance on my cattle, but surely I was right in trying to revenge him; now that we are both satisfied why should not we be friends again?"

"No, no," said the Serpent; "take away your gifts; you can never forget the death of your son, nor I the loss of my tail."

The moral of Aesops Fable: Injuries may be forgiven, but not forgotten.

Thoughts from Parents

Always be in the habit of hugging your son as he enters the house. This does more than assure your boy that you love him, it gives you the opportunity to smell him. Does he smell like smoke or alcohol? Do some research and find out which will be the best way for you to handle these problems.

Choose your son's friends. You may not be able to do this directly, but you can do it indirectly by encouraging him to hang out in places that will lift his educational and moral standards.

Acne and skin irritations are going to happen. The face, back, and buttocks are super sensitive. Usually cleaning gently with soap and then rinsing well using a non-soapy washcloth will help to rub away these problems. If the breakouts get bad go to a dermatologist early on. The longer you wait, the harder it will be to treat.

Want to be big and strong like Popeye? Eat your Spinach. Actually there is no one food that will make your boy stronger, but eating balanced meals will.

Have the evening meal together, at the table. No phones, no computers, no TV, just your family and friends. If that's not possible, make time to have a snack together, around the table.

Pumping iron is not good for young boys. They aren't going to get big muscles until they go through puberty anyway, so why let them take a chance on damaging themselves. The best way to build muscles is to play. They need to run, jump, ride their bike and play sports, anything that keeps them active.

Be strong and courageous. Do not be afraid or terrified because of them, for the LORD your God goes with you; he will never leave you nor forsake you. Deuteronomy 31:6

Chapter Twelve

When Tommy was twelve years old, he became very good in soccer. We had changed states during this time, and we put him in a Christian school, which we thought he'd do well in, but he didn't. He fought to keep his long hair and his jewelry, but during that time he became a very popular sports figure and he liked that. So the next year we put him back in public schools, and they had just started soccer, so he had a head start and always excelled in soccer. It is hard on kids when they have to change schools.

Del Grogg

When Del went to WVU, his English teachers told him he should be a writer; he has never pursued this occupation, but he often helps his wife Cher'ley on her projects. Now he has a couple of stories of his own to publish.

He enjoyed creating the stories and remembering his childhood. He doesn't remember being as rotten as some of his relatives remember him being.

A New Best Friend or a Hole More Shallow
by Del Grogg

"I'm tired." Bobby sat down right there in the middle of
the road. "And I'm hungry."

"You're a baby." I didn't want to admit my hunger, or my
fear.

"No, I ain't no baby. I'm the same age as you."

"You are too." I tugged on his arm. He was a baby. He
always acted like a baby. If I barely touched him, he'd start
screaming. If I hadn't been so tired myself I probably would have
found a way to have dumped him as my friend. Well, at least as
my best friend. I'm sure there were other five-year-olds in our
neighborhood who would have been happy to have been my best
friend. He was a whole month younger than me, and even
though he acted like a baby, he felt as big as an elephant as I
continued to tug on his arm.

"Get up. Get up. Get Up!" I screamed, as much as a
person could scream through clenched teeth. "You're going to get
us both kilt."

"You don't need to be here. I think you're a scaredy-cat."

"I'm not scared. You're stupid. You don't have the sense to
get out of the road. Get up, or I'm leaving you." At that moment
I was really mad at Bobby, still I didn't want him to get run over
by a truck or something.

"Your mom is going to be so mad."

"Yours' too." I snapped back at him.

I thought about Mom. I wanted her to know I was mad,
but I didn't want to get in trouble from her. I was already in
trouble from Dad. That was partially Bobby's fault too. I didn't
think of becoming a miner all on my own. As we sat in the hole,
Dad passed by us and said, "Fill that in."

That really made me madder than a hornet whose nest had
been torn down and set on fire with kerosene. It had been a lot
of work digging that hole, and I wasn't about to put that dirt
back. As soon as Dad was out of earshot I put my little chubby
fists on my hips and said, "I'm runding away. You with me?"

Bobby thought it was a grand idea and off we went. We didn't even take our cap guns for protection

I looked down at Bobby. He still would not budge. If he would get a move on, I could get home before Mom missed me.

And even if Mom already missed me, she'd probably think I was at the neighbors. Kids ran around in their own neighborhood without worrying that someone would kidnap them, 'speacially in *my* neighborhood, nearly everyone was family, or a shirttail relative.

I knew if Bobby would just get his butt in gear; I could at least make it home before dad. I started getting a vision of what would happen if Dad made it home before me.

It felt like we'd been gone for days, instead of the short time we'd been missing from my yard. We had crossed roads and gone up one side of a hill and come down the other side. The scariest part, the part where I just knew Bobby and I would both perish, was when we crossed the bridge used by the railroad. We'd walked up the railroad tracks in order to stay hidden from anyone who might be looking for us. It didn't look like it was that far to the other side of the bridge, but it was. The scary part-- and Bobby was just as scared as I was, if not more so—was as we crossed the bridge there were big spaces between the railroad ties. We could look straight down between the ties and see the water as plain as day. We never thought of the danger we'd be in if a train came that way while we were on the railroad bridge, but we both grabbed our chest in relief when our feet touched solid ground.

Finally, Bobby stood up and brushed off the seat of his pants.

He asked the question that I didn't want to hear. "Which way is home?"

I wanted to sit down in the middle of the road where Bobby had just gotten up from. I had grown more tired, hungry, and scared as the time ticked away. I knew we had to keep moving if we wanted to find shelter before dark, or even if we wanted to find our way home, because surely we had been gone all day. Nothing Dad could do to me could be as bad as being stuck out here after dark.

"Let's keep moving."

Bobby didn't answer for a few minutes. He had to stop sniffling first. He ran his arm, wrist first, up the tip of his nose and then whined, "I wanna go 'ome."

"Nah, we'll find somewhere to go, let's just keep moving."

We walked along shuffling our feet in the gravel. Not even one car had passed us, so all that worrying I'd done over Bobby getting kilt was for nothing. Suddenly I noticed a sign on a tall smokestack.

"Bobby look. We're in Texas." I didn't know all of my alphabet, but I could recognize a capital T. Renewed, we headed for Texas.

Before we could get all the way to the smokestack, my heart sank. There was the Lion's Market, the market where my mom and dad bought their food, and I could tell by the fit Bobby was throwing that his mom and dad shopped there too.

"We ain't in no Texas. There's the groceries store." He kicked the dirt and gravel up into the air, but that didn't bother me none.

"Then why's there a sign that says Texas?" I stuck my chest out with as much authority as I could muster, which wasn't much considering my dilapidated state of being.

Now Bobby was acting all brave, he rushed ahead of me into the market. He pointed across the road to the smokestack that was attached to the back side of the big, old, dirty factory, "Does that sign say Texas?"

"Bobby, what gave you that idea?" The lady said. "It says The Viscos. It's the name of the plant."

I figured if she knew Bobby's name; she knew mine too, so I backed out the door. I heard her asking Bobby where his Mom was. She said she didn't hear no car. I don't know how Bobby answered her, but he came out the door smiling.

"I know the way home."

"Oh yeah. How do you know she's not lying?"

"She's a grown woman, she can't lie."

That made sense to me. "Which way?"

"She said straight down that road. She wants Mommy to call her when I get home."

"Let's go." The smells coming from the market reminded me of how hungry I was. No matter how mad Mom was, she'd still feed me.

I felt relieved when Dad's car wasn't in the drive. Mom met us at the door.

She said, "Bobby, you better run along home. Your folks are looking for you."

Bobby skittered away.

By the look on Mom's face, I knew I was in a lot of trouble. She had one of those faces; the kind mothers have with a look for a different look for every situation. Right then it looked mighty angry. She grabbed me by the ear and said, "Let's get you into the tub and cleaned up. You look like something the cat drug in."

I yelped.

"Are you hurt?" She held me out away from her. She gave me the once over.

"No, you're hurting me."

She continued guiding me, by my ear, into the bathroom. "You're going to think you're hurt when your dad gets ahold of you."

By this time, I'm butt naked, and in the tub. I was still mad too. The thought of filling our mining hole back in angered me all over. I said, "If that old man thinks he's going to beat me, he has another think coming. I'll just run off again."

I no sooner had spoken those horrible words before the bathroom door flew open, and in entered my dad, belt in hand.

I'll never forget the green shower curtain that I wrapped around my body to help soften the blows.

He turned to my Mom. "Get him dried off and out in that yard filling in that hole. Now!"

So where was Bobby when I needed him, probably sitting down to a nice warm meal, while I slaved by myself, filling in the hole we had dug together. I wonder if I could have found a better best friend.

The Big Black Book
By Del Grogg

"You kids stop fussing, I'm too busy to chase after you today. Now hush before you wake your Daddy." Mamma yelled over the ruckus of her nine children ranging from the ages of eleven months to fourteen years old. The memory plays in my mind as vividly as if I was still an eleven-year old boy anticipating spending the whole day with my daddy.

"Calvin, get some more wood." Mamma said. The urgency in her voice came through loud and clear. The room became silent. The younger kids didn't seem to understand what Mamma was saying, but I knew this day had to be perfect.

My father worked all the time in order to take care of a wife, nine youngins and my grandfather, Old Pop. He labored on our small farm that was seated high up on Frog Mountain, but mainly he was a lumberjack. In addition to his other work, Daddy trapped for extra money. He also hunted and fished to put meat on our table.

Daddy was 6'4" and as wiry as a youth. I was fascinated as I watched him use his red, chapped hands to tack skins to a special made board. Even though his hands were huge, he used them gracefully, as if he were playing a delicate instrument.

I was almost old enough to go with Daddy on a hunting expedition. Willie, my older brother, had told me exciting stories about the trips he'd made with Daddy. They'd be gone for a week hunting and checking the traps. I could only imagine what it would be like to spend a whole week with Daddy. When he was home, he had so many chores to do around the farm that he'd rise long before the sun was up and not come into the house until way after dark. Sometimes I got to spend time with Daddy when he was home. But, mostly, by the time he finished his chores, I would be asleep. Daddy worked every day except for one day a year.

After I got the wood for Mamma, I sat by the window watching the snow and waiting for Daddy to get up. The wind whistled under the door. I yelped as a cloud of snow burst in through a big crack around the window.

"Calvin, grab me some of them scraps of bark over near the stove." Daddy's booming voice startled me almost as much as the burst of snow had. I scurried to fetch the bark. He used a big piece of flat iron to stuff the bark and rags into the gaps around the window frame to keep the snow and wind out.

Our house was just a little more than a cabin with three tiny bedrooms and a main room we called the "Big Room" because it was bigger than all the others. The big room contained the black iron cook stove, which sat close to the back door. Next to it was a large rough-hewn table with benches on each side. Two big chairs set at each end. Close to the fireplace set two wooden rocking chairs. One rocker was Daddy's and the other one belonged to Old Pop. Mamma had an upholstered rocker, and there was a long couch and a big chair.

Mamma and Daddy had one bedroom. Two bedrooms were split between the older girls and the older boys, the babies slept in Mamma and Daddy's room. Old Pop had a very small room in the back of the house.

I was born in that shack February 8, 1899. I don't remember sleeping in Mamma and Daddy's room, but I'm sure I did. All of us kids slept in Mamma and Daddy's room until we could walk.

My childhood days were filled with romping on the side of Frog Mountain and helping around the farm. One of my favorite pastimes was making fun of Old Pop. He was a frail and sickly man with little tufts of white hair on his head. He mumbled and grumbled all the time, which gave me plenty to make fun of.

"You kids be nice to Old Pop. He's the reason we've got this here land and this nice house. If'n it weren't for him hard tellin' where we'd be," Daddy often warned us. "You kids need to spend more time learnin' and less time funnin'.

Daddy worried a lot about our education. He said he wanted us to have a better life than he had, and that book learning was the key to getting off Frog Mountain. Mamma was well educated. She was going to be a teacher when she fell in love with Daddy. She wasn't from Frog Mountain--she was from what she called 'back east'. She came to Frog Mountain with her Mamm'a for a visit and never left.

"Give these youngin's a good ed-ecation, Martha." Daddy would say. Mamma would respond by going into their room and coming back with the big black book.

"It's time to do your three R's." Mamma would say. We would do our reading from the Big Black Book. We had to be careful with the book because its cover was cracked and fragile, the pages were thin and yellow with age. Mamma turned the pages as we read the exciting stories about Abraham, Isaac and Joseph. We read about far-a-way lands and people from different nations. Reading was my favorite of the three R's. But, Mamma said that arithmetic and writing were important too. We had flash cards for arithmetic and each of us had our own writing tablets.

It seemed like Mamma always worked hard cooking, cleaning and caring for her family. She worked harder on Daddy's day home than any other day of the year.

"Calvin go with James and get the turkey from the smokehouse. Susan and Jodie go to the cellar and get me a jar of cranberries and those peach preserves that your Daddy loves." I remember Mamma barking out orders to each of us. Finally, she put her hands on her hips and smiled really big as she looked around the room with approval.

Mamma smiled, and we giggled. Daddy sat in the rocker by the fireplace holding a burlap bag between his knees. As soon as everything was in place, Mamma nodded to Daddy. It was the signal we were waiting for.

"I found this bag. I wonder what's in it?" Daddy had teased. We all gathered around Daddy as he pulled gift after gift from that fat bag.

Mamma acted so happy when Daddy pulled her gift from the bag. She cried and held the brightly colored cloth close to her heart. Mamma made most of our clothes. When an older kid outgrew an item, she'd patch it up to hand it down to the younger kids. Material cost a lot of money, and she didn't get new bolts of fabric often.

Next Daddy pulled out Old Pop's gift. A new hat! Old Pop cackled and danced a little jig. Daddy gave us a stern look that

let us know not to say anything to Old Pop and then he dug into
the bag again. He gave the boys a toy horse, a toy pig, or a toy
cow, which he'd carved out of wood, and the girls got a doll that
Mamma made. We all laughed when Sara wanted to trade her
doll for Michael's horse.

With a big grin, Daddy started pulling out shoes. Little shoes,
big shoes, shoes of all sizes. Mamma let out a little gasp, and her
hand flew to her mouth. Daddy winked at her and whispered,
"Did a bit of bartering."

But, I was more excited about Daddy being home all day
than I was about the new shoes. I was standing close to Daddy
when he put his big hand on my head and turned me towards the
table. I licked my lips as I stared wide-eyed at the mounds of
mashed potatoes. Fresh baked bread. Deep dishes filled with
vegetables. And in the middle, a golden brown turkey!

Our little shack was warm and cozy that day. The meal was
as wonderful as it looked. I got a turkey leg all to myself. The
smell of fresh baked pies lingered in the air, but I was too full to
eat a piece. Mamma said not to worry because there'd be plenty
to have with milk at suppertime.

After dinner, Daddy went into their bedroom and brought out
the Big Black Book. He had what he called his marker, a thin
piece of leather with a cross scratched on it, between the pages,
towards the end of the book.

"Now we'll read a bit." Daddy's smile reflected the happiness
of the day. We older kids knew Daddy couldn't read. Mamma said
when he was growing up he didn't need to learn to read; all he
needed to learn was how to work. Our eyes turned toward
Mamma waiting for Daddy to hand her the big black book so she
could start reading. But, Daddy didn't hand the book to Mamma
he opened the book to where his leather marker was. He cleared
his throat.

"Long, long ago in a town far from Frog Mountain..." Daddy's
voice was soft and quiet. It grew in volume and strength as he
continued. "A girl was likened to have a baby. The fellow that
was a-courtin' her was mighty upset because they weren't
married yet. An angel came and told the fellow it was okay
causin' the baby was from God.

They lived way out, but it was an order from the law-keepers that they had to go to Beth-lee-ham to sign up in order to pay taxes. They had come a farce way and were tired. They needed a place in a hurry causin' the baby was coming. There was a big house where people could stay if'n they were from out of town, but it was full. The owner of the house said he didn't have any room, but they could stay in the barn. Right there among the cows, the horses, and the donkeys the baby was born. His name was Jesus, and He was the Son of God." Daddy bowed his head as he closed the big black book.

"It's a miracle." I said. Mamma and Daddy agreed with me, but I don't think they knew I was talking about Daddy being able to read the story.

After Daddy finished the story, we helped Mamma clean up, and I got to thinking how perfect the day had been so far.

"Why do we have Daddy's day just one day a year?" I asked Mamma.

"Oh Calvin, you ask that every year." she laughed. "It's not Daddy's day, it's Christmas. You know it's the day we celebrate the birth of Jesus."

"I know, Mamma, but wouldn't it be nice if we could have Daddy's day more than once a year?"

"Yes it would be nice." Mamma answered.

But, it never happened, every year Daddy worked every day except for that one special day. The time came when I was to leave Frog Mountain. Daddy said we needed to sow our wild oats before we came back to the farm.

So here I sit in France, deep in a trench, fighting and trying to stay alive. Bodies of young men lay all around, some of them remind me of my brothers. It's a cold day in December; the noise of mortar and rifle fire is deafening. Smoke and dust hang in the air like a thick fog. All at once the noise quiets and the smoke clears. I look up and see the stars. It dawns on me that it's that certain day. I think of Mamma and Daddy, my brothers, sisters, and that old shack on the mountainside. Oh, how I long to be in that beautiful, peaceful place.

I reach into my breast pocket pulling out my Little Black Book and in a soft, quiet voice I begin to recite, "Long, long ago in a town far from Frog Mountain..."

The Wind and the Sun
An Aesops Fable

The Wind and the Sun were disputing which was the stronger.

Suddenly they saw a traveler coming down the road, and the Sun said: "I see a way to decide our dispute. Whichever of us can cause that traveler to take off his cloak shall be regarded as the stronger. You begin." So the Sun retired behind a cloud, and the Wind began to blow as hard as it could upon the traveler. But the harder he blew the more closely did the traveler wrap his cloak round him, till at last the Wind had to give up in despair. Then the Sun came out and shone in all his glory upon the traveler, who soon found it too hot to walk with his cloak on.

Aesops Moral to the story. Kindness effects more than severity.

Thoughts from Parents

Education is very important. A boy needs to find out early on what he loves to do and find a way to get paid for his passion. The best years of his life are during the time when he is a boy.

Teach him to dance. Not just slow dancing, but fast dancing too. If you can't do this, find a young aunt, or an older cousin who can help. Have parties at home that include dancing. It's good for him to see his parents dancing.

Teach him to laugh, not at others, but with others and at himself.

He will have suffering in his life. Love ones will die. He will fail. People will disappoint him. These things he will have to experience. No matter his age a kiss from Mom can still make it better. A soft voice, and an understanding heart, and a strong shoulder to lean on will help to get him through his pain.

Encourage him to push himself to the max. Go places he normally wouldn't go. Try new things. Teach him to use all of his senses. Tell him to smell the roses, lay on his back and gaze at the clouds, taste the cold snowflakes as they fall on his tongue, sit outside in the early morning and listen to the birds, and feel the soft grass under his feet.

Give him a place to escape to. Help him to express love and to accept love.

Two things to help in the transition from boy to man:

(1) "A man never stands as tall as when he kneels to help a child."- Anonymous (2) "Small boys become big men through the influence of big men who care about small boys."- Anonymous

Blessed are those who find wisdom, those who gain understanding, for she is more profitable than silver and yields better returns than gold. Proverbs 3: 13, 14

Remember: When raising boys the days are long, but the years are short.